The Assassination of Walter Reuther

THE ASSASSINATION OF WALTER REUTHER

Why They Did It, How We Know

Rob McKenzie

Algora Publishing
New York

Library of Congress Cataloging-in-Publication Data
Names: McKenzie, Rob, 1952– author
Title: The assassination of Walter Reuther : Why they did it, how we know/ Rob McKenzie.
Description: New York : Algora Publishing, [2025] | Includes bibliographical references and index. | Summary: "In 1970, UAW President Walter Reuther died in a plane crash involving a private jet. No public hearing was held, the FBI did not investigate, and FOIA requests were stalled. Few who knew the man believed it was an accident. Newly uncovered documents provide solid evidence indicating the crash was an assassination."— Provided by publisher.
Identifiers: LCCN 2025020406 (print) | LCCN 2025020407 (ebook) | ISBN 9781628945720 trade paperback | ISBN 9781628945737 hardcover | ISBN 9781628945744 pdf
Subjects: LCSH: Reuther, Walter, 1907–1970 | International Union, United Automobile Workers of America (CIO) | Automobile industry workers—Labor unions—United States—Biography | Labor unions—United States—Officials and employees—Biography
Classification: LCC HD6509.R4 M35 2025 (print) | LCC HD6509.R4 (ebook) | DDC 331.88092—dc23/eng/20250703
LC record available at https://lccn.loc.gov/2025020406
LC ebook record available at https://lccn.loc.gov/2025020407
Description: New York : Algora Publishing,

Front cover:

Pellston crash site May 10, 1970.

"Battle of the Overpass, 1937. Henry Ford's security goons pummeled Walter Reuther and UAW staffers attempting to hand out leaflets."

Photos courtesy of the Walter P. Reuther Library, Archives of Labor and Urban Affairs, Wayne State University.

Printed in the United States

Table of Contents

Prologue

Four passengers converse in the dim cabin-area light of a Learjet 23 during the nighttime flight from Detroit to a small airport in northern Michigan near the city of Pellston. The group includes Walter Reuther, 62, president of the United Auto Workers union, his wife May Reuther, 59, renowned architect and Reuther family friend Oskar Stonorov, 64, and Reuther's bodyguard and May's nephew, William Wolfman, 29. Captain George Evans, 48, is flying the chartered private jet, and the co-pilot is Joseph Karaffa, 40. At 20 miles out from the Pellston airport, Evans talks with the Federal Aviation Administration Flight Service Station specialist Thomas Sorrick, the only person working there that evening. They review the weather, which was light rain and some wind. Evans notifies Sorrick that he will choose a runway approach upon arrival. When the craft reached the small airport, Evans began to circle the airport to land at an illuminated runway opposite their approach path for unclear reasons. That illuminated runway was the only one without flashing Runway End Identifying Lights, forcing Evans to rely on his altimeter to determine the jet's altitude.

As the craft nears the approach to the runway, it begins its descent. The pilot monitors his altimeter as they near the runway. At 9:33 p.m., the jet aircraft clipped the top of a large elm tree, sucking into its two engines debris composed of limbs and branches. At 145 m.p.h. this causes a flame-out. The aircraft sailed another ½ mile in the air before it crashed into a pine forest, exploding on impact. It erupted into a blaze of flames, and everyone on board was killed.

So ended the life of legendary labor leader Walter Philip Reuther. Four days after the May 9, 1970, crash, the Veterans' Memorial Building in Detroit was opened for mourners to pay their respects. People from around the world, including Europe, Australia, and South America, joined the rich and poor, black and white, old and young, who trooped past Walter's wooden casket adorned with the UAW emblem. Around 3,400 invited guests attended the farewell ceremony, while thousands more stood outside to listen to the speakers. Inside the auditorium, Hubert Humphrey, George Shultz, Henry Ford II, George Romney and Edward Kennedy joined those grieving Reuther's death. Additionally, 30,000 autoworkers remained away from work, and the Detroit Big Three (General Motors, Ford, Chrysler) automakers halted assembly lines for three minutes to commemorate Reuther.

The UAW established a legal tenor for a follow-up of the crash when the auto union didn't support a public inquest into the deaths at the Emmet County Airport. Leonard Woodcock, the officer who replaced Reuther after an internal union power struggle, based his decision on a memo written two weeks after the crash by the union's General Counsel, Stephen Schlossberg.

The National Transportation Safety Board issued its seventeen-page report eight months after the incident. It contains a great deal of data. The NTSB found the probable cause to be the pilot's inability to visually recognize how low the plane was because of darkness and a faulty altimeter that was likely to have been reading 225–250 feet higher than the aircraft was. The report inexplicably leaves out critical information from the altimeter manufacturer's investigation and examination that were issued the same day Stephen Schlossberg wrote his report to Woodcock. Yet independent journalists and historians have uncritically accepted the consensus opinion that this was an accident.

In 1985, Bill Gallagher, a Detroit reporter from a public television station, filed a Freedom of Information Act request with the FBI for documents on Walter Reuther. Gallagher persisted and after two years, the Bureau acknowledged having 8,400 pages of records, most of which were either redacted or withheld in their entirety.[1] There are some related to the Pellston crash. They, too, are heavily redacted, and the Bureau withheld some in their entirety. In 2022, I submitted my first request for FBI documents related to the Pellston incident. Initially, the Bureau denied my request, claiming no relevant records. However, after I presented them with files previously released to Gallagher in the 1980s, they discovered some documents and transferred my request to a Disclosure Analyst. In 2024, they released fourteen pages of records. These included six publicly available newspaper articles and four inconsequential correspondences I already possessed. They removed the redactions from four memos from the FBI's Detroit Field Office, all sent to Director Hoover within 24 hours of the crash. Other redacted documents released to Gallagher talked about a "contract" let on Reuther in the months before the plane crash; they raise concerning questions about the Federal Bureau of Investigation's involvement in Reuther's death, and the Bureau refused to declassify those.

In 1992, Walter's daughter Elisabeth was skeptical of the official explanation and she enlisted David Norris, a private investigator, to investigate the crash. In 2023, Norris told me there was a civil suit related to the crash, but he could not obtain the court documents. In 2024, I managed to get 1,286 pages of court documents from a civil suit filed by the Reuther Estate against the Emmett County Airport. These records, along with the recently relocated Kollsman Instrument report on the captain's altimeter, provide concrete evidence that the deaths in the Pellston plane crash were the result of an assassination.

Walter Reuther was a pivotal figure in American labor history. He served as president of the United Automobile

1 During negotiations over my FOIA request in 2023, the FBI informed me that another individual had requested declassification of all 8,400 documents, which were sent to a Disclosure Analyst. They estimated it would take six or seven years to process the request.

Workers from 1946 to 1970 and played a significant role in shaping the modern labor movement. He is unique among U.S. national union leaders in his dedication to workers' rights, social justice, internationalism, and civil rights activism.

Chapter 1. Early Years

Born on September 1, 1907, in Wheeling, West Virginia, Walter Reuther was raised in a family that valued social activism and union organizing. His father, Valentine Reuther, was a German immigrant and socialist union organizer who instilled in Walter and his siblings a strong sense of social justice and the importance of worker rights. The Reuther household was a place of intellectual discourse, with Valentine facilitating debates on social issues every Sunday for his sons. Valentine developed a close personal relationship with Socialist Party presidential candidate and labor activist Eugene Debs. Debs opposed entry into World War I, was convicted of violating the Espionage Act, and was sentenced to ten years in prison. The elder Reuther brought the boys to visit the incarcerated Debs.

The family experienced financial difficulties after Valentine suffered a severe eye injury while at work. Walter left school at sixteen and began an apprenticeship as a tool maker at a local factory. In 1927, at nineteen years old, Walter moved to Detroit. He secured a job at the Ford Highland Park plant within a few months. He later transferred to the River Rouge facility and worked at Ford for five and a half years. At the onset of the Great Depression, Walter's younger brother Victor joined him in Detroit in 1930. They rarely spent time apart for the next five years and developed a strong bond while collaborating on political and union activities.

In 1932, Ford laid off Walter. In 1933, he left the country with Victor, announcing, "We are going to study the economic and social conditions of the world." They arrived in Germany in time to witness the Nazis take complete control while their socialist friends went into hiding. Using a relative's home as a base, they toured Europe. They biked through France and into Italy, then visited Austria and England. Their travels through Europe confirmed their anti-fascism and pushed them towards left-leaning political views. They became convinced that the Soviet Union was a necessary bulwark against the spread of fascism, so they applied for a visa to visit there. In November 1933, the visa was granted, and the Reuther brothers traveled to Moscow and then on to Gorky, where they worked in an auto plant for eighteen months.

Ford Motor Company played a significant role in the development of Gorky's automotive works. The item most sought-after by the Soviets was the small mobile Fordson tractor, and 20,000 of them had been sold to the new government during the 1920s. The Soviets were keenly interested in having Ford train a cadre of Russian technicians to build a Model A equivalent. When Walter was working at the River Rouge plant, fifty Russian trainees worked there. According to Victor, in line with the Stakhanovite movement (promoting workers who excelled in applying the new mass-production techniques), Ford was considered a hero in the Soviet Union, "nearly as respected as Marx and Lenin." Henry Ford was deeply committed to supplying practical assistance to the Soviet people, not just for commercial reasons. During this time, he was promoting international peace.[2]

Ford reached an agreement with the Bolshevik government on May 31, 1929, to ship 72,000 knocked-down Model A vehicles to Russia over three years, train Soviet technicians in Detroit, and send experts to Russia to supervise the tooling of the new Gorky facility. The exchange of technicians began in 1931. When

2 Victor G. Reuther, *The Brothers Reuther and the Story of the UAW/A Memoir* Houghton Mifflin 1979 p. 91

the first car rolled off the assembly line, the Russian workers tossed the Ford production expert in the air with a blanket like a hero. The production process had just begun when Walter and Victor arrived.

En route to Work: Victor and Walter at the Gorky Automotive Works in the Soviet Union in 1934. Walter is on the right.

The Reuthers worked in the tool room at the massive Gorky auto complex. They trained Russian peasants to begin industrial work for the first time. The 1930s were difficult years for the Soviet Union. To underwrite the costs of a major national industrialization program they were forced to export an appalling amount of their national wealth, and the campaign to collectivize agriculture did not go well. Although they were offered more generous allowances as foreign workers, Walter and Victor did not take advantage of that arrangement but ate in the cooperative cafeterias instead of the special restaurant for foreigners. They became aware of the privations that the workers endured. They participated in the Soviet *subbotnik*, or volunteer labor projects, that were declared whenever an "emergency" came up — like completing a school or hospital. These projects were organized by trade unions or youth groups and included music, dancing, and extra food as well as some hard work.

The Reuther brothers lived in the American Village with thirty other U.S. technicians. The area became very popular, and girls from villages all around found excuses to come to their social evenings. That is how Walter met Lucy. Victor described her as beautiful, graceful, and educated. With their limited Russian, Walter and Victor invited her to attend the next party. Walter saw Lucy frequently and finally went to meet her parents. Victor went along to interpret as his Russian was better. The relationship grew into a full-fledged love affair. Victor moved out of their room, allowing Lucy to move in, turning their bleak cubicle into a home with curtains, pictures, needlework cushions, and fresh flowers. Walter had pledged to Victor and Roy that he would not get married on the trip as he had expected to lead a life of hardship on his return doing serious union organizing work. Walter reassured Victor that he had not changed his view and that he had an understanding with Lucy that they would enjoy the relationship without a permanent commitment.[3]

The Reuthers witnessed the transformation of a feudal society into an industrial state. They were astonished at the progress and the rise in the standard of living but disheartened at the price society was paying. With the assassination of Kirov

3 Ibid. pp. 107-109

in 1934, Stalin's purges began. Victor saw Kirov as a remarkable and unpretentious man who had rapport with both intellectuals and workers. Stalin and his allies blamed Trotsky for the killing, but Victor didn't see any evidence for this; the event was used as an excuse for launching an enormous purge. The purges reached into the Gorky factory, and the workers quickly lost their individual freedom. The brothers returned to the U.S. through Japan and China.

Still, for the first two and one-half years back on U.S. soil, Walter was enthusiastic about Soviet achievements and the character of the new society.[4] But Walter and Victor would eventually become vocal critics of the Soviet regime.

Meanwhile, the Great Depression had devastated the US auto industry, leading to widespread layoffs and reduced wages. By 1932, Detroit's unemployment rate was between 30% and 50%. Many autoworkers faced unstable employment, with factories operating at reduced capacity or shutting down altogether. Work was seasonal and unstable, with no guarantee of being called back after layoffs, and many workers were forced to bribe foremen. Those who retained jobs often saw their wages slashed. Even full-time workers struggled to make ends meet. Many families lived in overcrowded conditions due to their inability to afford housing. Thousands fell behind on rent and house payments, facing eviction, homelessness, and exposure. Many families struggled to survive on donated food baskets, and some people in Detroit died from starvation while malnutrition was prevalent during the winter of 1932-1933. Factory working conditions were brutal, characterized by intense speeds on assembly lines and arbitrary power given to foremen to hire and fire workers.

Upon their return to Detroit in early 1935, the Reuthers found the New Deal had somewhat transformed the city. Walter rejoined the Socialist Party and began working with the Socialist Auto Council, which supported an industrial trade union structure. Walter dedicated himself to organizing the large number of auto workers in the area. He attended the AFL convention

4 Nelson Lichtenstein, *The Most Dangerous Man In Detroit: Walter Reuther and the Fate of American* Labor p.44 Basic Books 1995, p. 44, *The Brothers Reuther and the Story of the UAW/A Memoir* pp. 99-110

in 1935 when the Committee for Industrial Organizations was formed. The CIO was born out of a fundamental dispute within the U.S. labor movement over how to organize industrial workers. Its founders were dissatisfied with the AFL's unwillingness to work with America's manufacturing industries and its focus on organizing only skilled craft workers.

The Communist Party had adopted the Popular Front strategy and was open to collaborating with socialists, so Walter worked with them in the union organizing effort. There is some inconclusive evidence that Walter may have joined the Communist Party, an allegation that followed him throughout his life. FBI Director J. Edgar Hoover portrayed him as a closet communist disloyal to his country. The FBI collected a massive file of 8,400 documents of rumor, hearsay, and fantasy and circulated this whenever his name came up for a government position.

Walter began seeing May Wolf, a vibrant young teacher he met in the Socialist Party. Most of their time together had been at union meetings, and the courtship was less than glamorous. May's parents were Jewish immigrants from Russia, and Walter had known her father from Socialist Party activities in the early 1930s. They were married on March 13, 1936, and spent their honeymoon at a labor rally. They would have two daughters, Linda and Elisabeth.

The American Federation of Labor (AFL) supported the organization of the United Automobile Workers in 1934 but did not allow delegates to elect their officers. The AFL president, William Green, appointed these officers. At the 1936 South Bend convention, delegates were in a belligerent mood and won the right to elect their officers. Walter was elected to the Executive Board of the newly autonomous union.

In 1936, Walter won election to the Michigan UAW's executive board. Walter had been blacklisted in Detroit and was unable to find a job, but Kelsey Hayes Wheel hired Victor. Shortly after, the workers at Kelsey Hayes Wheel engaged in a sit-down strike for union recognition, improved wages, and shorter hours. The company eventually conceded, but another sit-down strike began at the General Motors plants in Flint, Michigan, before Kelsey and the UAW signed the final agreement.

On December 30, 1936, a sit-down strike commenced at a GM Fisher Body plant in Flint, soon spreading to a larger plant in the city. Victor was one of the UAW organizers and actively participated in the strike. He helped coordinate food and supplies for the striking workers occupying the factories. He played a crucial role in spreading information and rallying community support. Later, during the famous "Battle of the Running Bulls" on January 11, 1937, Victor was involved in efforts to defend the striking workers when police attempted to break the occupation. One of the activists was another Reuther brother, Roy, who was also a key UAW organizer. He helped strategize and mobilize workers for the occupation. He worked alongside his brothers and other union leaders to sustain the strike and build momentum for union recognition.

"Battle of the Overpass," 1937: During the infamous "Battle of the Overpass," Henry Ford's security goons pummeled Walter Reuther and UAW staffers attempting to hand out leaflets to workers at the Dearborn, Michigan, complex. In the widely photographed encounter, the UAW leaders were beaten, and several were seriously injured.

Walter Reuther and Richard Frankensteen, with swollen faces after the "battle." The press coverage and photographic evidence of the violence turned public sentiment against Ford, helping to galvanize support for labor rights. Although Ford held out longer than other automakers, this event marked a turning point in labor organizing in the auto industry, with Reuther and Richard Frankensteen, another vice president of the UAW at the time, playing key roles

Walter called a sit-down strike at a Cadillac plant in Detroit, and by the end of January, 125,000 GM workers were on strike. With the intervention of Frank Murphy, Governor of Michigan, and Committee of Industrial Organizations (CIO) head John L. Lewis, GM agreed to a settlement recognizing the UAW as the bargaining representative for the union members at the twenty GM plants on strike. The UAW's victory in Flint was decisive in establishing industrial unions in America. In 1937, UAW membership surged to over a quarter million.[5] The win over GM began the most energetic and tumultuous union organizing in the nation's history.[6] By the end of March, Detroit cigar makers,

5 Lichtenstein, *The Most Dangerous Man In Detroit* p. 74

6 John Barnard, *American Vanguard. The United Auto workers during the Reuther Years, 1935-1970*, Wayne State University Press 2004. p. 95

meat packers, servers, and clerks had all sat down, and in the country at large, 500 sit-down strikes had taken place, one of the most extensive civil disobedience outbursts in the nation's history.

Walter Reuther took on the role of director of the UAW GM Department in 1939. He was elected vice-president in 1942 and became UAW president in 1946, a position he held until his death. Throughout these years, various organized factions vied for power and leadership within the union. These factions were divided by political, ideological, programmatic, and ethnic conflicts, as well as personal ambition and, to some extent, trade union issues. These tumultuous years would greatly influence Reuther's perspectives on organized factions and internal dissent within the union.

Chapter 2. Factional Conflicts

During the 1936 UAW convention in South Bend, Indiana, delegates removed the principal official appointed by the AFL president. Walter emerged as a leader of the majority progressive faction, consisting of socialists, communists, and urban radicals from ethnically and racially diverse constituencies. Another faction, primarily composed of white Protestants of northern European descent from smaller towns and cities, distrusted the progressives. This conflict would reemerge repeatedly in the coming years.[7] The factions reached an agreement, selecting Homer Martin, a Baptist minister, as president and Wyndham Mortimer, a communist, as vice president.

After the strikes in Flint and the GM agreement, Martin created a right-wing faction called the Progressive Caucus and started opposing the radicals who formed the Unity Caucus. To solidify his control over the union, Martin needed to attract intellectuals to help run it. For this assignment, Martin enlisted Jay Lovestone, a former Communist Party member and leader of an anti-Stalinist communist sect (Lovestonites). He would become a lifetime Reuther foe.

Jay Lovestone arrived in New York City with his Russian immigrant family in 1906. As a young man, he became immersed

7 Lichtenstein, *The Most Dangerous Man In Detroit* pp. 105-113

in the radical politics of the time. Using a talent for factional maneuvering and working behind the scenes, he rose to become the head (general secretary) of the American Communist Party by the end of the 1920s. During the 1930s, the general secretary and other American communists became engulfed in the infighting that enveloped the Soviet Communist Party. Lovestone had aligned himself with Nikolai Bukharin, the head of the international communist organization the Comintern. Bukharin was a figure who stood in Stalin's path to complete power in Soviet Russia. Stalin's fight against Bukharin was eventually successful, and it resulted in Bukharin's execution in 1938.[8]

Lovestone and ten other Americans had received orders to go to Russia for meetings in 1929 during the fight that was raging between Stalin and Bukharin. There, Stalin removed Lovestone as general secretary of the American Party. He allowed the other Americans to leave but forced Lovestone to stay. With a friend's help, Lovestone escaped Russia. Upon returning to the U.S., he organized the American Communist Party Opposition (Lovestonites), but by the middle of the 1930s, he had become intensely and personally anti-communist.[9]

Still, Lovestone continued his mission to organize American workers to fight for better employment terms. He focused on the International Ladies Garment Workers Union, where one of his followers, Sasha Zimmerman, ran for union office. In 1933, with Lovestone's help, that Lovestonite became president of the largest local in the ILGWU (International Ladies Garment Workers Union) and one of the largest local unions in the U.S. The International President of the ILGWU, David Dubinsky, recognized Lovestone's talents and his potential for fighting communists.

In 1937, Dubinsky, a relative conservative in the newly organized CIO and the International Ladies Garment Workers Union president, sent Lovestone $100,000 to help Homer Martin fight the communist influence there.[10] Lovestone became Martin's chief of staff for two years and devised a strategy to drive the

8 Ted Morgan, *A Covert Life Jay Lovestone Communist, Anti-Communist-Spy Master* Random House, 1999, pp. 48–66.
9 Ibid., pp. 105–112.
10 Ibid., pp. 110-124

communists out of UAW leadership. In 1938, Martin suspended four communist-aligned executive board members. Walter led a walkout of six other board members in protest.

Lovestone wholly controlled Martin, as a union trial of the four expelled UAW executive board members would later prove. Martin fired dozens of staff members in addition to the suspended international executive board members. A target was the Flint GM local, where, along with others, Martin fired Roy Reuther. Victor was transferred out of Detroit and then dismissed. Victor's wife, Sophie, was also fired. He replaced them with loyalists.

The three brothers, Walter, Victor, Roy Reuther.

In the weeks following the expulsions from the IEB, unknown people robbed an apartment Lovestone was using under an alias, and they stole important papers concerning the UAW. A few days later, at the union trial of the suspended board members, the attorney representing the ousted board members offered the stolen papers in evidence to show Lovetone was manipulating Martin. John L. Lewis had seen enough and ordered Martin to reinstate the barred board members. Martin refused, and Lewis suspended the UAW from the CIO. Following a UAW convention in 1939, Martin took his followers (about one-fifth of the UAW) into the AFL. After a year, that effort collapsed, and all those members returned to the UAW-CIO. In more recent times, after the dissolution of the Soviet Union in 1991, the new Russian government opened Comintern files in Moscow to researchers, and those proved that the Soviet State Political Directorate (GPU), the secret police agency of the Soviet Union which operated as a part of the NKVD, had been responsible for the burglary of Lovestone's papers.[11]

In the summer of 1939, the UAW organized a five-week strike involving skilled tool and die makers across General Motors (GM) plants in Detroit, Saginaw, and Cleveland. This strike is often regarded as a pivotal moment in American labor history, particularly in the automotive industry. As head of the GM Department of the UAW, Reuther led the strike. Left to Right: Victor Reuther, William Stevenson, Walter Reuther, Robert Pitt. 1939.

Lovestone's attempted coup incurred the Reuthers' lasting hatred. Walter saw Lovestone as his foremost implacable enemy,

11 Ted Morgan, *A Covert Life Jay Lovestone Communist, Anti-Communist-Spy Master* Random House, 1999 p. 129

and their feud continued when he became UAW president and Lovestone directed AFL-CIO international affairs. The mutual loathing did not end until Walter's death at the Emmett County Airport.[12]

While working as director of the Free Trade Union Committee, Lovestone was recruited as a CIA agent in 1955 by the Agency's counterintelligence chief, James Angleton, who ran him through an aide, Stephen Millet, who also had the Israel desk. Angleton managed payments to Lovestone through New York lawyer Mario Brod.[13] Upon learning of the Lovestone operation when he became a new CIA director in the 1970s, William Colby assigned a trusted officer, Horace Feldman, to investigate Angleton's activities. Feldman told Colby:

> Here we have a senior officer in the labor movement, a domestic organization outside our mandate, and he is in our pay. And he publishes a newspaper, the Free Trade Union News. This is a clear violation of our charter. Lovestone is collecting information on U.S. citizens.[14]

After Colby forced Angleton out in 1975, he assigned his successor the task of reintegrating the counterintelligence staff into the CIA mainstream. In his review of Angleton's office, he found the JX Files, reports from Lovestone. The fact that Lovestone had been an agent was not even known to the Agency's labor division.[15]

When AFL-CIO president Meany discovered in 1973 that Lovestone was receiving payment from the CIA, he forced him out as the organization's international affairs director.[16] A former AFL-CIO International staffer told me that Meany didn't have a problem with the CIA, but he was a stickler for money and didn't want his employees to get double pay.

---

12 *Ibid.* p. 132

13 Tom Griffin, *State-Private Networks and Intelligence Theory From Cold War Liberalism to Neoconservatism.* Routledge 2022. p. 70

14 Morgan, A Covert Life, p. 349

15 Hugh Wilford. *The CIA: An Imperial History*, Basic Books 2024, p. 189

16 Jeff Schuhrke, *Blue Collar Empire: The Untold Story of US Labor's Global Anti Communist Crusade* Verso 2024 p. 221

The growth of anticommunist sentiment in the country and the UAW contributed to the breakup of the Unity Caucus in 1938. Reuther began to distance himself from the communists as he drew back from some of the radical positions he held during the depth of the Depression. The Communist Party dumped Reuther as a partner and allied with a former Homer Martin ally, Dick Frankensteen. The split was completed in the Michigan State CIO convention when the consensus Unity Caucus candidate for secretary-treasurer, Victor Reuther, was deserted by delegates affiliated with the CP on instructions from the party. Walter responded with a declaration of war and threatened to "drive you bastards out of the union." The open hostility and the fight with the Communists became a significant theme in UAW history.[17] The factional strife resulted in the loss of union membership and threatened the existence of the UAW.

Reuther's bitter fight with the Communists from 1946 to 1949 led him to oppose all organized opposition in the UAW and adopt autocratic measures to accomplish this. The factional debate was functionally prohibited. After Reuther's death, his former caucus became a self-replicating oligarchy. When the UAW began moving politically to the right, its suppression of any dissent accelerated the union's embrace of company/union jointism and its descent into corruption, nepotism, and incompetence.

Victor Reuther joined with New Directions, a UAW opposition movement, in the 1980s, to challenge the former Reuther Caucus, which had become the Administrative Caucus. A dissident assistant region director, Jerry Tucker, led the New Directions movement. Tucker lost his election for the position of region director by a margin of 0.16 votes out of a total of 650 cast at the 1986 UAW convention (delegates have voting power proportional to the size of their constituency). The Department of Labor found that some delegates were elected improperly and ordered a new election. In the new election, Tucker won with 52 percent of the vote. Aided by Victor, Tucker challenged UAW president Owen Bieber and his caucus on the issues of the cooperative programs that the Big Three auto companies

17 Barnard, *American Vanguard.* pp. 131-133

wanted. He also advocated more rank-and-file participation in the union. Reuther and Tucker were very critical of Bieber and his caucus's tactics, which they believed to be undemocratic. At the 1989 UAW convention, Tucker and another candidate for region director were defeated, and the New Directions movement was overcome.[18]

The UAW was reinvigorated when the federal government indicted many high-ranking officers on corruption charges and mandated a referendum to decide the question of continuing with the delegate election system or switching to a direct membership voting system. The direct membership election prevailed. A small opposition group, UAWD, helped form a slate that defeated many incumbents, including the president, in 2023. (Appendix I)

18 John Holusha, "Union Rebel. Jerry Tucker—The Man Who Is Fighting the U.A.W. from Inside," New York Times, October 23, 1988. I was active in New Directions and was elected on a New Directions platform as a convention delegate from UAW 879 to the 1989 national convention. I met Jerry Tucker and Victor Reuther in this context.

Chapter 3. World War II

Nazi Germany and the Soviet Union signed a pact in 1939 which facilitated a coordinated attack on Poland by these countries. With that, Reuther's factional conflict with the Communist Party entered a new phase. On September 29, 1939, Germany and the Soviet Union formally partitioned Poland between them. The Communist Party in the U.S. spurned the Popular Front strategy and supported an anti-war isolationist agenda. A host of socialists, radicals, and liberals who had worked with the CP denounced their former allies and, along with thousands who left the Party, began to organize pro-war sentiment in support of the British. Also in 1939, the ideological Cold War began, and it continued for the rest of Reuther's life and past his death.[19]

The outbreak of the war in Europe and the Red Army's move into bordering countries also changed the political alignment of many working class families, especially ethnic Finns, Poles, and immigrants from the Baltic States of Estonia Latvia and Lithuania. They had previously supported unions and the left, but came to hate the Soviet Union and its supporters. The German invasion of the Soviet Union less than a year later did little to change this. At a UAW convention in 1940, Reuther allies passed a resolution (Victor was a contributing author)

19 Lichtenstein, *The Most Dangerous Man In Detroit* pp. 154-158

condemning "the brutal dictatorships and wars of aggression of the totalitarian governments of Germany, Italy, Russia, and Japan."[20] Reuther emerged from the 1940 convention as a political equal to all others in the UAW leadership and a spokesman for the pro-defense, pro-Roosevelt segment of labor.

The U.S. began full-scale defense mobilization following Roosevelt's 1940 re-election to his second presidential term. Roosevelt called for a tripling of defense spending and a peacetime draft, and the United States provided over $31 billion in military aid to Britain through the Lend-Lease Act of 1941. To meet these goals, Roosevelt needed to reach accommodations with his erstwhile opponents in corporate America. For example, General Motors controlled 10 percent of the nation's entire manufacturing capacity. Things did not go smoothly. There were long delays in conversion to military production. Even when conversion was embraced, it proceeded erratically. Critics of the auto industry claimed that manufacturers had held back from conversion to produce cars for as long as possible because the profits had begun to be good.

In May 1941, Roosevelt established the National Defense Advisory Commission, the first of several economic agencies to plan for war mobilization. Reuther was appointed to a manpower committee on the commission and used this position to promote his ideas of making Detroit the new center for aircraft manufacturing. Reuther met with UAW President Thomas and CIO President Murray and proposed converting the auto industry's unused capacity into one massive aircraft production unit. He called his plan "500 Planes a Day." Murray presented the plan to Roosevelt, saying:

> Believing again that labor is entitled to play an important part in our nation's well-being, some three months ago, I asked Mr. Walter Reuther, in association with a group of expert mechanics and tool and die makers who are members of the Automobile Workers' Union to make an exhaustive study of the ability of the automobile industry to produce airplanes. I had in mind the use of existing facilities plus preparation of new dies

20 Ibid. p. 157

> and tools to produce airplanes with a minimum of delay. Mr. Reuther and his associates have now submitted to me such a program, which I have enclosed.

Roosevelt responded positively, telling the Office of Production Management, "It is well worth our while, I think, to give a good deal of attention to his program."[21] Reuther's vision included giving workers a role in the re-tooling process; it was widely supported by the workers but opposed by the auto and aircraft companies, who feared giving the workers a say in matters that had been the exclusive domain of management. FBI Director Hoover agreed with the assessment of military intelligence that this was merely a plot to transfer nonunion aviation work to UAW plants in which the Communist Party had a strong voice. Walter and Victor were given a place on the FBI's "custodial detention" list of people slated for arrest should the president declare a national emergency. Hoover would be a Reuther enemy for the next 30 years.[22]

After Pearl Harbor, the government banned civilian auto production and feverishly began issuing contracts for the military. Reuther's plan was dead, but he won a seat at the table in Washington. In addition to the War Production Board, he had roles in the Office of Production Management and the War Manpower Commission, where he actively advised on wartime labor issues. The UAW made many sacrifices during the war, including a no-strike agreement for the duration and wage controls. Despite these, the real wages of auto industry workers rose by 20 percent. The war brought about the most rapid and significant redistribution of income in favor of blue-collar workers in the twentieth century.[23]

During these years, the war and Reuther's role as a leading spokesman for labor helped establish a link between union rights, patriotism, and economic progress that would last far into the future. Reuther pushed for integration of the defense workforce, challenging racial discrimination in war industries. He supported A. Philip Randolph's call for fair employment and

21 Reuther. *The Brothers Reuther* p.226
22 Ibid. pp. 166-167
23 Barnard. *American Vanguard.* p.179

helped lay the groundwork for the Civil Rights movement. His success in negotiating a contract between GM and the UAW that emphasized the social responsibility of the auto companies toward its workers led to his election as president of the UAW in 1946, a title he held until his death.

Walter Reuther speaking at a May Day Rally in Berlin. May 1, 1959.

Chapter 4. Legacy

In 1948, Walter was shot through a window in his home by an assailant using a twelve-gauge shotgun from nine feet away. One arm was shattered and nearly severed. Surgery and years of physical therapy led to a partial recovery of its use. In that attack, another shot hit him in the back and exited the front of his body. Although large rewards were offered, the murder attempt was never solved.

Thirteen months later, Victor Reuther was shot through his living room window and lost his right eye. When pressed to have the FBI investigate, Director Hoover replied that he would not open a criminal investigation "every time some nigger woman gets raped."[24]

Although large rewards were offered, neither murder attempt was ever solved. A mobster involved in gambling operations in auto plants was the prime suspect, but no one was ever charged in the case. In January 1954, a Detroit prosecutor obtained a confession from Donald Ritchie that he had participated in Walter's shooting at the behest of a gangster named Santos "the

24 Ibid. p.257. Lichtenstein, *The Most Dangerous Man In Detroit* p. 274. Hoover's statement is the version the UAW General Counsel Joseph Rauh gave. Rauh approached Attorney-General Tom Clark about getting the FBI involved in the shootings. He reported, "Edgar says no. He's not going into the South every time some nigger woman gets raped."

Shark" Perrone, a Sicilian mobster who was afraid the UAW would interfere with his gambling operations in their plants and his lucrative scrap metal contracts with the Briggs Corporation. But Ritchie escaped to Canada and subsequently renounced his confession. No one was ever convicted of the attacks on the Reuther brothers. Victor suspected the police were complicit.[25] In 1968, the State of Michigan extended the statute of limitations when it appeared there might be a break in the case.

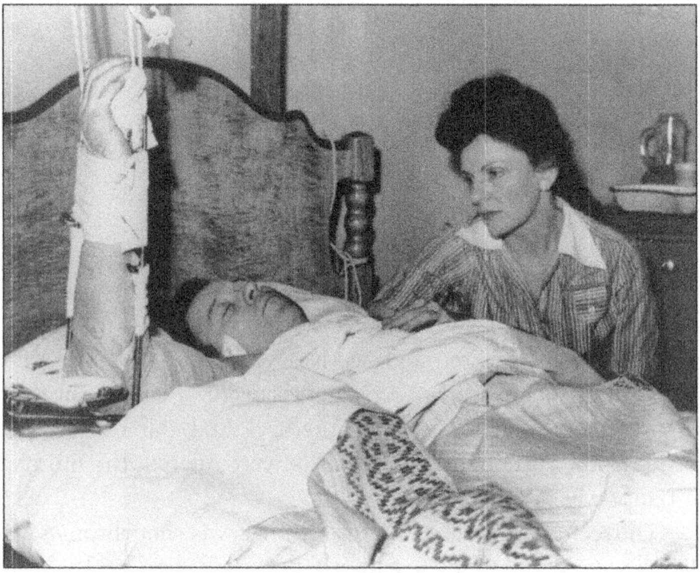

Walter has been shot; May Reuther is by his bed.

There were several high-profile political assassinations during the 1960s. President John Kennedy was murdered by rifle fire while riding in an open car in 1963. Following the assassination attempt on Reuther, the UAW purchased an armored Packard sedan, and Reuther only traveled in closed hardened vehicles. Then Sen. Robert Kennedy was killed in 1968. Not so well known is the fact that Thomas Noguchi, the Chief Medical Examiner and Coroner for the County of Los Angeles, concluded that the fatal shot was to the back of Kennedy's head, behind the right ear, at an upward angle, and from no more than 0.5 to 3 inches away. The assailant convicted of killing Kennedy, Sirhan

25 Reuther, *The Brothers Reuther* pp. 269-291

Sirhan, was in front of Kennedy, firing at a distance no closer than one meter (39 inches).[26] Walking slightly behind RFK was Thane Eugene Cesar, who was working as an Ace Security guard at the Ambassador Hotel on the night of June 5, 1968. He was standing guard over the room where Kennedy was ambushed and had taken Kennedy by the arm when he walked by. Cesar was seen with his pistol unholstered, standing over Kennedy. A witness told police he had seen Cesar fire the weapon. Police never closely examined Cesar and or his pistol, and he soon disappeared. He had previously made anti-Kennedy comments and said he voted for George Wallace in 1968.[27]

Walter Reuther never traveled without trusted bodyguards, so he would not be an easy assassination target in the future.

After establishing secure control of the UAW in 1949, Reuther made significant advances in collective bargaining. As a socialist, Reuther had hoped to use government action to obtain social benefits like health care and retirement security for the workers. The rightward turn of American politics after World War II drove unionists to negotiate these goals through collective bargaining and union contracts. The Reuther-led UAW won pensions for workers with 30 years of seniority, employer-paid health insurance, annual wage increases based on productivity improvements, and a cost-of-living allowance (COLA), ensuring that workers' earnings kept pace with inflation. He sought to win a Guaranteed Annual Wage and won Supplemental Unemployment Benefits for workers on layoff. These agreements marked a significant shift in labor relations, as they tied workers' well-being to long-term economic sustainability. Autoworkers moved up to the lower middle class.

An Era of Security, Benefits and Civil Rights

From 1945 to 1970, American autoworkers experienced **one of the most significant improvements in living standards in U.S. labor history**, establishing themselves as a cornerstone of the **postwar middle class**.

26 William Klaber and Philip Melanson, *SHADOW PLAY The Unsolved Murder of Robert F. Kennedy*, St. Martin's Press, 2018, pp. 98-99

27 Shane O'Sullivan, *Who Killed Bobby: The Unsolved Murder of Bobby Kennedy*, SkyHorse Publishing 2018 pp. 315-340

1946 – The UAW demanded a 30% wage increase without raising car prices. After a 113-day strike at GM, workers won a 17.5% wage increase.

1950 – The "Treaty of Detroit" (GM Agreement) established a landmark five-year contract with General Motors. It introduced cost-of-living adjustments (COLA), enhanced pensions starting at $125 per month, health insurance with GM paying half, and a 20% wage increase over five years, becoming a model for contracts throughout the auto industry.

1955 – Supplemental Unemployment Benefits (SUB)were introduced in the Ford contract. Ford's agreement brought new provisions for health and safety.

1958 – The Agreement featured wage increases and job security provisions. The UAW negotiated a guaranteed annual wage (GAW) at Ford and GM, which provided income security for laid-off workers and enhanced pension benefits.

1961 – The first major Employer-Funded Supplemental Unemployment Benefits (SUB) Agreement was won. This agreement with major automakers guaranteed ongoing income for workers during layoffs. When combined with government unemployment compensation, SUB allowed laid-off workers to collect up to 65% of their regular take-home pay.

1964 – Groundbreaking civil rights protections were negotiated. The UAW contracts explicitly prohibit racial discrimination in hiring and promotions. This contract also included significant wage increases and expanded health and pension benefits. Early retirement provisions were first introduced in the Chrysler contract.

Reuther believed that the emergence of a determined and militant civil rights movement in the 1960s could restart momentum for political reform and social justice. He threw himself and a sometimes hesitant UAW membership into the effort. The union provided critical funds for the Montgomery, Alabama, bus boycott, endorsed the lunch counter sit-ins, provided bail money for the freedom riders who were violently attacked trying to desegregate southern buses, and underwrote voter registration drives.

In 1963, the UAW donated $100,000 to the Southern Christian Leadership Conference, Martin Luther King's organization. Attorney General Robert Kennedy asked Reuther to lead the effort to raise bail money for the 840 civil rights demonstrators arrested in Birmingham, Alabama. The UAW was one of the ten official sponsors of the 1963 March on Washington for Jobs and Freedom. Five thousand rank-and-file UAW members attended. Walter Reuther was the only white labor leader to address the crowd and chided the Kennedy Administration for its slow progress on civil rights.[28]

UAW in Freedom March (anti-KKK), May 31, 1965, at Saint Mary's Dominican College.

In a perilous battle over voting rights, marchers were brutally attacked in Selma, Alabama, in 1965. In response, supporters thronged into Selma. One of them, a Unitarian minister, was beaten to death. Walter and May Reuther led a UAW delegation of 2,000 to a memorial service in Selma. Reuther was battling with many in his own union's membership who opposed these actions. Local 34 in Atlanta sent a petition to the executive

28 *American Vanguard.* pp.386-388

board signed by over half the membership objecting to Reuther's participation in civil rights demonstrations.[29] The Selma events culminated in the passing of the Voting Rights Act several months later.

Coretta Scott King, who had marched with Reuther, delivered a eulogy at his funeral.

> Walter Reuther was to black people the most widely known and respected white labor leader in the nation. He was there when the storm clouds were thick. We remember him in Montgomery. He was in Birmingham. He marched with us in Selma and Jackson, Mississippi and in Washington.... Only yesterday, there he was once more in Charleston, South Carolina, the leader of a million and a half workers giving personal support to a strike of only 400 black women...He had the courage to be with the minority when it was right. He was a simple man in his personal life, a rare quality in these flamboyant times...but if his ways were simple, his ideas were grand. He aroused the imagination of millions...[30]

The American Institute for Free Labor Development

In 1949, pro-Western unions formed the International Confederation of Free Trade Unions (ICFTU) in opposition to the World Federation of Trade Unions, the Soviet-backed international labor federation. The American Federation of Labor was determined to make the question of totalitarianism the primary focus of the new organization. At the same time, European socialists and social democrats wanted to emphasize social justice and economic security. The Europeans had an ally in this, Walter Reuther. During the coming decades, Reuther and AFL president Meany would stake out opposite poles within the anti-communist labor consensus.

Victor and Walter believed that the Free Trade Union Committee, the foreign affairs arm of the AFL run by Jay Love-

29 Ibid. pp. 403-404

30 Elisabeth Reuther Dickmeyer, *Putting the World Together My Father Walter Reuther: The Liberal Warrior*, LivingForce Publishing, 2004. P.351

stone, was receiving large sums of money from the CIA. (The agency may have given it two million dollars annually between 1949 and 1958.)[31] When the AFL and the CIO merged in 1955, Reuther tried unsuccessfully to remove Lovestone.

In 1962, the AFL-CIO collaborated with the Department of State and intelligence agencies to establish the American Institute for Free Labor Development. Reuther supported an organization made up of labor and academics. However, when Meany secured funding from government sources for AIFLD, Reuther distanced himself. Victor had harbored suspicions about AIFLD since its inception. In the fall of 1961, Victor wrote to Walter expressing his concerns regarding the nine months' pay that AIFLD training graduates would receive upon returning home, stating, "Each of them will not only be vulnerable to accusations from our opposition that they are agents of the U.S., but they will also clearly be compensated by a U.S. institution that includes employers and government in what is presumably a 'labor training' program." Since AIFLD became the sole U.S. government-backed labor program in Latin America, Victor perceived it as "very nearly a private, unregulated, and irresponsible monopoly."[32]

AIFLD established training centers in Brazil at the end of 1962. The first group of 33 Brazilian labor leaders arrived at the AIFLD training center in Front Royal, VA, for training in January 1963. Their six-month course included classes in U.S. labor history, economics, and techniques for combating communism and fascism. Follow-up surveys revealed that many of the Brazilian leaders were largely unimpressed, and U.S. officials, frustrated with the training, were eager to support a long-planned coup d'état. In April 1964, the democratically elected president of Brazil, João Goulart, was overthrown by a CIA-backed military coup. Serafino Romualdi, AIFLD Executive Director, was aware of the coup's planning. Deposed President Goulart was a member of the Brazilian Labor Party and enjoyed widespread support from workers and the trade union movement in Brazil. When the coup began, the Brazilian Communist Party called for a general strike. AIFLD-trained unionists were positioned to

31 Schuhrke, *Blue Collar Empire* p. 75

32 Carew, *American Labour's Cold War Abroad*, pp. 257–264.

effectively divide labor, urging the communications workers to remain on the job. Their directives kept communication systems operating, enabling the military to coordinate and seize power.

Workers were at the center of conflicts in the Goulart government, and it would be accurate to characterize the coup as one staged against workers.[33] When the military seized control in Brazil, they put army officers in charge of unions; they abolished the right to strike, and opposition dissidents were imprisoned and, in some cases, tortured. Following the takeover, communist-led unions were put into trusteeship and purged of leftists and Goulart supporters. Labor contracts negotiated during the Goulart government were allowed to be terminated by employers. In the aftermath of the coup, AIFLD representatives began advocating for a wage freeze proposed by the military regime. The AFL-CIO embraced the new regime and bragged about bringing it to power.[34]

Victor Reuther attended the first meeting of the Labor Advisory Committee (composed of representatives of the Departments of State, Labor, and Defense, the CIA, the U.S. AID, the U.S. Information Agency, and the AFL-CIO) held in May 1964 after the coup. He raised questions about the ethics of labor's role in the events in Brazil. Although he was at the meeting in an unofficial capacity, he heard reports about AIFLD doubling their activities and coordinating with officials from the Department of State (DoS). Andrew McClellan, the AFL-CIO Inter-American Regional Organization of Workers (ORIT) representative, defended the new Brazilian government's practice of intervening in unions as "necessary to provide continuity in legal counseling and social welfare services."[35]

Three months after the coup, William Doherty Jr., then AIFLD director of the Social Projects Division, gave an interview on an AFL-CIO sponsored radio program. When asked, "What happened to these individuals who learned the techniques and

33 Paulo Fontes and Larrissa R. Corrêa, "Labor and Dictatorship in Brazil: A Historiographical Review." Published online by Cambridge University Press, May 3, 2018, p. 27.

34 Schuhrke, "Comradely Brainwashing," pp. 60–62.

35 Welch, "Labor Internationalism," pp. 84–85.

programs of Free Trade Unionism [the AIFLD training program] in recent developments?"

He replied:

> Well, very frankly, within the limits placed on them by the administration of João Goulart, when they returned to their respective countries, they were very active in organizing workers and helping unions introduce systems of labor-management relations. As a matter of fact, some of them were so active that they became intimately involved in some of the clandestine operations of the revolution before it took place on April 1. What happened in Brazil on April first did not just happen—it was planned—and planned months in advance. Many of the trade union leaders—some of whom were actually trained in our institute—were involved in the revolution and in the overthrow of the Goulart regime.[36]

Victor was furious about AIFLD's involvement in the Brazilian coup. After similar events in the Dominican Republic in 1965, he urged Walter that the UAW should withdraw from the AFL-CIO. Walter agreed that the CIA was using the labor movement to disguise covert activities. However, he doubted that Victor could provide sufficient evidence to withstand the onslaught of fabricated documents and lies that the CIA might produce to counter such a claim. Walter opposed forcing a split with the AFL-CIO over foreign policy when their focus was on domestic issues. The conservative craft unionism of the AFL often conflicted with the CIO's liberalism, and he believed a better opportunity would arise soon.

And it's true that taking a strong public stand on that issue would have left the union vulnerable to criticism. Even so, an attack was made in 1965 when the UAW was involved in a union organizing drive at Airmold Products in Tonawanda, New York. The company was owned by the Grace Company, whose CEO, Peter Grace, had recently become chairman of the AIFLD board. The company mounted an all-out attack against the UAW and

36 Reuther, *The Brothers Reuther* p. 419.

the concept of unionism. Their anti-union literature included criticism of unions' funds being spent to help international unions. The Grace Company leaflets said, "Do you want to pay dues to help finance foreign unions in foreign countries? Ask the paid organizer about this private foreign aid program."

Walter strongly opposed the involvement of corporate executives in AIFLD, and the Tonawanda incident provided him an opportunity to act against AIFLD. Although he was aware that government funding was also a factor, he focused his criticism on corporate contributions. He resigned from the AIFLD board that same year. Victor had been pondering what to do about AFL-CIO, AIFLD, and the CIA for quite some time. In an interview in May 1966 with the *LA Times*, Victor, who was the head of the UAW International Affairs Department, suggested there were ties between AFL-CIO foreign policy, AIFLD, and the CIA.[37] In the article, he gave eight individuals in Panama who were posing as representatives of the International Union of Food and Allied Workers, an International Trade Secretariat, as an example of CIA meddling. They had been doing this without the knowledge of that organization's general secretary, who was forced to abolish their Panama office and its entire Latin American operations as a result. Andrew McClellan hired these mysterious "representatives." Reuther asserted that the AFL-CIO International Affairs Department was "involved" with the CIA, and they had not reported much of that activity to the executive council.[38]

The reaction to the 1966 *LA Times* article was immediate. Joseph Beirne of the CWA, who had managed the pre-AIFLD training prototype and served as the AIFLD secretary-treasurer, along with Meany, called Victor's remarks "a damned lie." After a contentious executive council meeting in June, Walter was promised a thorough discussion of the AFL-CIO's Latin American operations at the August executive council meeting. However, before that meeting, Walter received phone calls from both Vice President Hubert Humphrey and former Attorney

37 "CIA Linked to AFL-CIO Foreign Unit," LA Times–Washington Post News Service, May 23, 1966.

38 Harry Bernstein. "V. Reuther Links CIA, AFL-CIO," Washington Post, May 23, 1966.

General Robert Kennedy, who urged him to stop the conflict over AIFLD. Walter criticized Victor for publicly addressing the CIA. He believed he had reached an understanding with Meany through his top aide, Lane Kirkland, to keep AIFLD off the agenda for the sake of national security, and that Meany had agreed to this during a face-to-face meeting. Walter prepared for the August executive council meeting by having his staff investigate AIFLD. In July, UAW General Counsel Joe Rauh wrote to Walter Reuther and reported the conclusions of the research:

> Since I know you are mulling over the CIA matter, you are entitled to have this thought before you. We can demonstrate, all apart from George Meany's admissions to you personally, that there is a massive CIA involvement in the foreign affairs operations of the AFL-CIO and vice versa.... [M]y personal assessment, based on what we have learned to date [is] that Vic's statement was mild indeed and that you can lead from strength, not weakness.[39]

When Walter got to the August meeting, Beirne attacked Victor in the first item on the agenda, comparing Victor's words to the "slanderous line of the Commies." Beirne made a motion to denounce the "campaign of vilification that has been waged against AIFLD." The resolution passed with a 23–2 vote, with only Walter and Joe Curran of the Maritime Union opposed.

The resolution declared:

> The Executive Council commends the American Institute for Free Labor Development for their work in carrying out the policies of the AFL-CIO in the international field and rejects out of hand the campaign of vilification that has been conducted against the AIFLD.[40]

In 1975, ex-CIA agent Phillip Agee named Beirne an important CIA collaborator in the labor movement.[41]

That meeting was the last straw for Walter, who, with the approval of the UAW executive board, initiated a process of

39 Ibid., p. 270.
40 Romualdi, *Presidents and Peons*, p. 431.
41 Agee, *Inside the Company*, Appendix 1, pp. 623–624.

leaving the AFL-CIO. In February 1967, he resigned from the AFL-CIO executive council. An item carried by Solidarity magazine for February '67 is entitled "To Clarify UAW's Position with the AFL-CIO." It's a text of an administrative letter sent to all the UAW locals by the four top officers at the instruction of the executive board. It says, "The AFL-CIO lacks the social vision, the dynamic thrust, the crusading spirit that should characterize the progressive modern labor movement." The process was completed in 1968 when the AFL-CIO suspended the UAW for nonpayment of dues, and the UAW executive board voted to disaffiliate.

In 1948, Paul Schrade dropped out of Yale to visit California and subsequently took a job at North American Aviation in Inglewood, an airframe factory contracted for Cold War military production. By 1951, he was president of UAW Local 887, which represented several thousand employees at the plant. Employers in Southern California's aerospace industry were determined to keep wages well below those secured by the major industrial unions back East. In 1953, Schrade led a contentious 53-day strike at North American Aviation that resulted in significant wage increases. In the late 1950s, Walter Reuther recruited Schrade to work as one of his assistants in Detroit. Schrade became a critic of the anti-Communist prohibitions enforced by the UAW and other unions during the Cold War. His commitment to civil liberties strengthened even more when, in 1962, he returned to California as the director of the UAW's 90,000-strong West Coast Region. He believed in the intersection of labor rights with broader struggles for equality and democracy.[42]

Paul Schrade remembered the debate in the UAW over foreign policy and the CIA:

> THOMAS CONNORS [interviewer]: They were older socialists [UAW officers] who had been around since World War II, so they had a whole very different point

42 Nelson Lichtenstein, Harold Meyers "The Autoworker Who Transformed California," *The American Prospect* November 25, 2022

of view from George Meany and Jay Lovestone and Irving Brown. That created a debate on foreign policy within UAW.

PAUL SCHRADE: Within the UAW [international executive] board. Most of it had to do with the ILO [International Labor Organization] and the International Confederation of Free Trade Unions. There had also been Victor [G. Reuther]'s exposure of the CIA [Central Intelligence Agency] involvement in a lot of the AFL-CIO's overseas activities and the kind of reactionary regimes that the AFL-CIO was supporting along with the government, which always seemed to us a contradiction. Because Meany's attack on the unions in the so-called communist countries was that they were government controlled, and yet here, at the same time he was accepting money from the [United States Department of] State and AID [Agency for International Development] and involving himself with the CIA and corporate leadership in this country to involve himself in Third World countries. It seemed to be somewhat the same thing, only an American version of this kind of government involvement with the unions in overseas activities. So all of that kind of gelled into a position of our talking about leaving the AFL-CIO. Walter was concerned at that point with making it too much of a foreign policy point. So his other criticisms of the AFL-CIO became more of the basis for our discussions about the policies of the AFL-CIO, which finally led to our break because he was concerned about organizing activities, collective bargaining activities, and so forth. There's a lot of paperwork on this. There's a real exchange going on.[43]

The attacks on Victor for exposing the role of the CIA in AIFLD were not limited to labor. In a May 1967 edition of the *Saturday Evening Post*, Tom Braden, a retired CIA official who

43 UCLA Library Center for Oral History Research. Interview with Paul Schrade. Tape X Side One June 5, 1990

was a top assistant to CIA Director Allen Dulles between 1951 and 1954, wrote an article entitled "Why I'm Glad the CIA Is 'Immoral.'" It appeared to be a defense of CIA operations in private U.S. organizations. Braden also seemed to cross a line by discussing CIA agents operating in a cultural organization and a journalistic publication. However, his article contained new information: as chief of the International Division of the CIA, he had given Walter Reuther $50,000 in 1951, which he, in turn, provided to Victor to spend on behalf of anti-communist unions in West Germany. The article caused Victor much embarrassment and further criticism. Victor admitted to doing it but also recounted Braden's effort to recruit him as a CIA agent who would play the same role Irving Brown was doing for the AFL-affiliated FTUC. He declined the offer.[44]

Reuther speaking at a Ford Rally at Cobo Hall, Detroit, in 1967. The UAW conducted a 68-day strike against Ford that year (one of its longest strikes against a major employer).

While Braden's article gave the impression of unauthorized action by a partisan, it is more likely that he proceeded with the foreknowledge of the CIA, who were aware of the impending

44 Thomas W. Braden, "Why I'm Glad the CIA Is 'Immoral,'" Saturday Evening Post, May 20, 1967, pp. 10–14; Reuther, *The Brothers Reuther*, p. 423.

publication and had ample time to invoke Braden's secrecy oath. The Johnson administration had prior knowledge about the article before publication. It was a common tactic for the CIA to expose covert operators who were no longer useful. The Reuthers' actions against AIFLD had put them in that category.[45]

It is easy to criticize Walter for not withdrawing from the AFL-CIO sooner. From the organization's inception, it was clear that internal democracy within the merged entity was a farce. At almost any point, he could have brought his many conflicts with Meany to a head and left the Federation. These conflicts included important policy issues such as organizing, civil rights, and international labor relations but also extended to matters like meetings held at resort areas and playing cards at Executive Council meetings. Beyond his conflicts with Meaney, by the late 1960s, Walter had become concerned that the movement for social and economic justice, propelled by industrial unionism, had begun to stall. Unions created under the National Labor Relations Act of 1935, which were based on representing workers with a common employer, reached their membership peak as a percentage of the workforce in the 1950s. Reuther's concerns about the labor status quo took organizational form.

On July 28, during the tumultuous year of 1968, Reuther established a rival labor federation called the Alliance for Labor Action (ALA). Reuther's vision for the new organization was based on the idea of a "community union." In 1967, Walter wrote:

> A new concept of union organization has been developing in areas such as Delano and Watts, California. Properly nurtured and motivated, it can spread across the face of the nation, changing the social character of the inner-city structure and uplifting the lives of millions of inner-city slum dwellers. This new organizing effort is called "community union." It is designed to provide the poor with their own self-sufficient economic organization.... Community cuts across many areas of social and economic need...health care, schools, public transportation, sanitation, building maintenance, etc. These and

45 Wilford, *The Mighty Wurlitzer*, pp. 244–247.

> many other facets of community life become integrated in the work and effort of "community unionism."[46]

The new organization included the Teamsters, the Chemical Workers, and, according to Paul Schrade, the Rubber Workers had joined at one point. The ALA represented four million union members. The alliance with the Teamsters temporarily stopped the jurisdictional warfare between them and Chavez's United Farm Workers union. Schrade, who had advocated for leaving the AFL-CIO for years, had been in negotiations with the California Teamsters over the alliance on June 5, 1968, the day Robert Kennedy was assassinated. The ALA provided organizing support for AFSCME, District 65 of the Wholesale and Retail Workers, and the Packinghouse Workers. Latinos in East Los Angeles organized with ALA assistance into a community group called TELECU. Similar efforts were begun in the inner cities of Newark, Chicago, St. Louis, and Daytona Beach, Florida.

At this time, the determinedly anti-communist AFL-CIO was vigorously asserting its support for the war in Vietnam. On May 8, 1970, Peter Brennan, president of the AFL-CIO-affiliated Building and Construction Trades Council of Greater New York, carefully planned and coordinated the infamous "Hard Hat Riot." About 1,000 young antiwar activists had responded to New York City Mayor John Lindsay's call for a "day of reflection." They were in Lower Manhattan peacefully protesting the killings at Kent State University earlier in the week. Two hundred construction workers marched into the protesters from all directions and, using their tools as weapons, began beating the antiwar demonstrators, chanting "USA all the way" and "Love it or leave it!" Police officers at the scene allowed the attack to go on unimpeded.[47]

In contrast, the ALA opposed the war and lobbied against its expansion. Paul Schrade believed that Teamsters president Frank Fitzsimmons took a hardline position against the war in the Alliance for Labor Action because Fitzsimmons's son was about to be drafted into serving in the military in Vietnam, so he had a personal interest in the issue. After Walter's death,

46 Reuther, *The Brothers Reuther*, p. 380.
47 Schuhrke, *Blue Collar Empire* pp. 185-187

the ALA dissolved, and the Teamsters established a close alliance with Richard Nixon. They joined with the fruit growers to launch one of the most violent strike-breaking campaigns in modern U.S. history against the Farm Workers Union.

After Reuther's death, visionary, out-of-the-box thinking about the mission and role of organized labor would be rare and infrequent.

Chapter 5. Last Years

The UAW made great efforts during the 1960 election to support John F. Kennedy, delivering 73% of UAW voters to Kennedy. Jack Conway, a Reuther aid, remembered Robert Kennedy, the JFK campaign manager, "used to say flatly that the UAW was the spine of the whole thing." After winning a close election, Reuther had great hopes Kennedy would pursue a liberal agenda supported by the UAW.

Reuther often functioned as a left flank just outside the administration. After the disaster of the Bay of Pigs, Kennedy enlisted Walter and Victor to negotiate with Castro over the release of 1200 captives. The Reuthers formed a "Tractors for Freedom" Committee and sent a UAW Region Director to Havana to negotiate. The plan fell apart after Republican criticism, but Castro later agreed to a financial settlement for the release.[48]

Victor was in Tunis when he learned of JFK's assassination in 1963.

> "Those bastards." I burst out. "They've finally killed him." There flashed before my mind bitter memories of the hatred and prejudice that had been nourished and broadcast across America for so many years. I real-

48 Lichtenstein, *The Most Dangerous Man In Detroit.* pp. 356-357

> ized then that I had always been afraid of exactly this moment.

The day after JFK's assassination, the new president, Lyndon Johnson, called Walter and said, "My friend, I need your friendship and support now more than ever before."[49] The 1965 session of Congress produced some of the most progressive legislation in the U.S. since the New Deal, but for Walter, like others drawn into Johnson's circle, a price had to be paid. The dearest cost for Reuther was support for the administration's war in Vietnam.

Reuther still depended on Johnson's backing to pursue his collective bargaining program. The UAW conducted a 68-day strike against Ford in 1967 (one of its longest strikes against a major employer). As momentum against the War increased, Reuther vacillated through the late winter and spring of 1968, saying he expected to vote for Johnson but maintained ties with the doves. The Americans for Democratic Action endorsed anti-war candidate Gene McCarthy, and Johnson asked labor leaders to resign. Reuther thought the endorsement was a mistake but stayed on. Reuther's reluctance to criticize the war provoked strong protests from associates, including his brother Victor.

On March 16, 1968, Robert F. Kennedy announced he would run for president on an anti-war platform. The UAW executive board split on an endorsement, with Walter advocating for Johnson. The California UAW Region director Paul Schrade announced he was joining convention delegates pledged to Kennedy in California. Reuther fumed at Schrade and demanded he withdraw from the RFK slate. Schrade charged the UAW was as detached and ineffectual as the AFL-CIO in helping resolve the moral issue of the war. On March 19, in a contentious executive board vote, Leonard Woodcock, the biggest hawk on the IEB, joined with Schrade and RFK, and they prevailed.

In an interview years later, Schrade recalled this IEB meeting:

> And also on the next day, when Reuther challenged me again on this [Schrade's support for RFK] because Vice President Hubert [H.] Humphrey and Lyndon Johnson had called him that morning before the board meeting at home and tried to get him to move to get me

49 Reuther, *The Brothers Reuther* pp.446-447

> out of the Robert F. Kennedy campaign—that's when I declared my position that I was not only endorsing Kennedy but was going on the delegation—none of that appears in the international executive board minutes. All of it was taken down by the court reporter. There was never any agreement by the board that that be deleted, yet it's obvious that it's there because there are references to the subject in a few statements about adopting the agenda in this board meeting. So, again, dealing with history is a difficult problem in a bureaucracy.[50]

Officially, the UAW stayed neutral, but every board member was free to support the candidate of their choice. Twelve days later, on March 31, LBJ withdrew from the race. Johnson's decision to terminate his candidacy was undoubtedly influenced by the UAW's de facto rejection of his presidency.[51]

Four days later, on April 4, Martin Luther King Jr. was assassinated in Memphis, Tennessee. The man convicted of King's assassination, James Earl Ray, was a career criminal who had escaped from the Jefferson City, Missouri, penitentiary in April 1967. After King was shot, Ray fled to Toronto and then to Portugal and England, where authorities apprehended him two months later while he was trying to board a flight to Brussels. At his trial, Ray pleaded guilty and received a sentence of 99 years in prison. Three days after his sentencing, Ray fired his mob-connected attorney, Percy Foreman, claiming he was pressured into pleading guilty and that he had been set up as a patsy.[52]

On June 5, Robert Kennedy was assassinated. Paul Schrade was walking with him in the Ambassador Hotel after the California primary victory and was hit by the first (or second) bullet fired in the ambush. He maintained his whole life that there was a second gunman involved in the killing of RFK.

---

50 UCLA Library Center for Oral History Research. Interview with Paul Schrade. Tape X Side One July 24, 1990

51 Nelson Lichtenstein, Harold Meyers "The Autoworker Who Transformed California," *The American Prospect*, November 25, 2022

52 Jeremy Kuzmarov. "Did J. Edgar Hoover Order the Assassination of Martin Luther King Jr?". Covert Action Magazine, April 4, 2004

Immediately after the RFK assassination, Walter Reuther agreed to co-chair the National Committee for a Political Settlement in Vietnam/Negotiate Now! It advocated an immediate cease-fire, including a bombing halt, positioning an international peacekeeper corps in Vietnam, free elections in South Vietnam, including participation by the National Liberation Front (Viet Cong), and land reform. Reuther planned to meet with Hubert Humphrey, the presumptive Democratic presidential candidate, and get him to adopt this position. They met on June 16 and June 24, but Humphrey was non-committal.

As the 1968 election drew near, Reuther became concerned that conservative forces were mustering to reverse the gains of the 1960s and the labor-liberalism he had worked so hard for. The right-wing, racist, populist George Wallace was attracting support among white UAW members. The UAW poured a half million dollars into the anti-Wallace campaign and assigned six hundred staff members to a nationwide effort to deny union votes to Wallace.[53] The effort won most of the union's vote for Hubert Humphrey, but an old Reuther enemy, Richard Nixon, was elected.

One month before the election, Walter and Victor flew to Washington D.C.'s Dulles International Airport in a chartered Executive Aviation Learjet. The weather was foggy on October 6, 1968, with light rain at 11:35 pm. As the plane came in for a landing, the pilot saw they were much too low, and the aircraft struck a steel girder. Victor described the impact at landing:

> As the pilot leveled, there was a jolt, the plane shuddered, and when the wheels touched, there was a loud dragging and scraping sound.... The plane whipped from side to side, nearly capsizing, but the pilots held it to the runway until it had slowed sufficiently to allow them to maneuver it onto the soft surface of an open field.... We could see that we had struck a steel girder as we landed: some four feet of it were rammed into the tail section and another six feet projected from the tail section to the ground.[54]

53 Lichtenstein, *The Most Dangerous Man In Detroit* p. 428
54 Reuther, *The Brothers Reuther*, p. 458

The hard landing damaged the jet's nose structure, gear well, and radar and navigation units in the front of the plane. The National Transportation Safety Board's Aircraft Accident Report on the mishap at Dulles blamed a faulty altimeter.[55] On the drive into Washington, DC, from the airport, Walter said, "I guess this wasn't intended to be our time."[56]

With Nixon's ascension to power, Reuther escalated his opposition to the War in Vietnam. In 1969, he endorsed U.S. withdrawal from the war-ravaged country, unilaterally if necessary. In October, the UAW supported the massive antiwar demonstrations of the Vietnam Moratorium Day with full-page newspaper ads and financial contributions.

All of this did not go unnoticed at Hoover's FBI. An FBI memo dated January 30, 1969, titled "Walter Reuther-Security Matter — Communist," was sent to C.D. Brennan, Chief of the FBI's Internal Security Section, whose work in the FBI at the time included efforts to track and apprehend members of the Weather Underground, a revolutionary group which operated clandestinely. The Bureau redacted the author's name and the memo's contents. Copies of the memo and an accompanying enclosure were sent to the Bureau's Internal Security Section and the Research Satellite Section.[57] The Internal Security Section of the FBI was responsible for investigating and countering activities it perceived as threats to national security within the United States. This section focused primarily on espionage, sabotage, subversion, and other forms of internal threats from both foreign and domestic sources. During the late 1960s, the FBI monitored groups suspected of being aligned with communist or socialist ideologies. The FBI maintained extensive surveillance and counterintelligence operations on these organizations.

In the 1960s, UAW members received good wages and benefits; now, some of them owned homes and other properties. They

55 Factual Aircraft Accident Report-General Aviation, Dulles International Airport, October 6, 1968, NTSB Accident Investigator, F.M. Fox. quoted in Richard Wiles, "Union man killed in Pellston plane crash: Accident or Conspiracy?" First published in the May 2015 issue of the *Mackinac Journal*. *The Brothers Reuther* p. 464

56 Reuther, *The Brothers Reuther*, p. 458

57 WJBK-TV Collection: Walter Reuther's FBI Files; FBI FOIA release No. 275,050; File No. 61-9556, Section 8, 1967-1970.Walter P. Reuther Library, Wayne State University, Detroit, MI

became increasingly conservative, and some younger members credited corporations for the gains that the UAW had won. The union sought to counter this with union education. Walter's last great project was creating a family education center in remote northern Michigan. Reuther envisioned the center to be aligned with nature. He asked his longtime friend and renowned Philadelphia architect, Oskar Stonorov, to design the new buildings at the proposed center.

Oskar Stonorov, modernist architect and architectural writer

Oskar Stonorov was a German American architect, sculptor, and urban planner known for his innovative contributions to modernist architecture and affordable housing design in the United States. He played a significant role in mid-20th century American architecture, particularly in housing and urban design. He died alongside Reuther and his wife May in the Pellston crash.

Born in Frankfurt, Germany, Stonorov studied in Paris and Zurich before emigrating to the U.S. in 1929. He was a pioneer in integrating social responsibility into architecture, focusing on housing projects that improved the living conditions of low-income communities. Stonorov was also deeply involved in the labor movement, designing the UAW Solidarity House. Completed in 1951 in Detroit, this served as the headquarters for the United Auto Workers union.

Stonorov designed the buildings at the UAW Family Education Center at Black Lake. Reuther and Stonorov wanted the education facility to be a lesson on building without destroying nature. Some say that Reuther personally examined and tagged practically every tree on the site to determine whether it stayed or was sacrificed for the center's buildings. Reuther conceived it as a vacation and living experience that would facilitate the study of the labor movement based on the values of community and democracy.[58]

Angie Stonorov Foster is a professional actress who has performed on Broadway, off-Broadway, and in regional theaters. She specializes in leading clowning facilitation. She is the youngest of the four Stonorov children. Angie recounts that the Reuther and Stonorov families were close, so she knew Walter and May from a young age. Lisa (Elisabeth) was her age, and they cherished one another. Lisa later called Angie her soul mate. May would read a story with the children before bed when the Stonorovs visited. One Christmas, when the children were much older, both families gathered at Black Lake. There were snowmobiles and outdoor fun. One of Angie's most prized memories is of all the family members standing around the piano singing union songs, with Walter leading, and probably her father at the piano.

Lisa, Walter's daughter, recounts in her book *Putting the World Together: My Father Walter Reuther, the Liberal Warrior* (2004) the Reuthers' and Stonorovs' get-together at Black Lake at Christmas in 1969. After caroling around the fireplace, the troupe marched around the snow-covered grounds of Black Lake with Walter and Oskar in the lead. Walter wore a red hard

58 Barnard, *American Vanguard*. pp. 457-458.

hat given by the Black Lake construction workers. It bore the letters CABGF — an acronym for Chief Architect, Builder, and General Flunky. Unknown to all, this would be Walter, May, and Oskar's last Christmas.

Stonorov Foster went to Selma in 1965. She was 18 and a freshman in college. She had some previous conversations with Walter about it, but:

> I ended up getting in a car with five strangers in Chicago and driving down. I felt so confident that I would see Walter when I got there. Instead, they were all in Brown's Chapel chanting and waiting for Walter and Martin Luther King to arrive in a helicopter. When she could, she went to the concrete building where Walter was waiting before speeches were given during the first march in the town. I went to the door of the building and explained that she was a friend of Walter's and was swiftly turned away with no hope of seeing him. Walter and she talked about it later, and being there at the same time was a bonding experience.[59]

On April 21, 1969, the FBI Field Office in Detroit received an anonymous call from an unknown male. The caller reported that a "contract" had been let on Walter Reuther. The name of the person the contract had been let to is redacted under exemptions 6 and 7(c) to the Freedom of Information Act. Exemption 6 involves individual privacy, and 7(c) protects individuals engaged in or mentioned in law enforcement investigations from having their identities or personal information revealed if it could be harmful or overly intrusive. The memo says that the Bureau advised Reuther's security staff of this. The Secret Service Headquarters was notified that the FBI had no references to the individual's name. The memo stated that there was no FBI jurisdiction.[60] (See Appendix II.)

Although the FBI claimed no jurisdiction, the Detroit office prepared an LHM, FBI code for a background check. on the same

59 Emails with Angie Stonorov Foster

60 WJBK-TV Collection: Walter Reuther's FBI Files; FBI FOIA release No. 275,050; File No. 61-9556, Section 8, 1967-1970.Walter P. Reuther Library, Wayne State University, Detroit, MI Appendix II

day in April. (LHM stands for "Letterhead Memorandum" in FBI terminology; it is a formal internal document used for various purposes, including summarizing background investigations, intelligence reports, and case updates. When used in the context of a background check, an LHM typically contains findings and conclusions from an investigation into an individual or organization.) The memo showed that it was sent to Director Hoover and ten other FBI employees, including W.C. Sullivan, the head of the COINTELLPRO program.

The FBI's COINTELPRO (short for Counterintelligence Program) was a covert and often illegal program initiated by the FBI in the mid-1950s to surveil, infiltrate, discredit, and disrupt domestic political organizations deemed subversive. The LHM was also sent to the Secret Service and G-2 (Military Intelligence). It was not sent to the Reuther staff. The memo was released to Bill Gallagher in 1987, but the LHM enclosure was not. In the memo's margin is a handwritten notation, "1d." Section 1(d) is an exemption to the Freedom of Information Act. It refers to materials whose unauthorized disclosure would reveal details about intelligence sources or methods, military operations, or foreign relations critical to national security.[61] (See Appendix II.)

A final memo on this subject was written on December 10, 1969. It was addressed to the same C.D. Brennan, whose work in the FBI included efforts to track and apprehend members of the Weather Underground. The subject was "Walter Reuther-Internal Security-Labor Matter." The author's name and the contents have been redacted. Only the final sentence was declassified. It states, "ACTION: The above information and enclosure are being directed to the attention of the Internal Security Section." It identifies three enclosures. The main body was redacted, and perhaps the enclosures were because it was "referred to another government agency for consultation."[62]

61 Ibid.

62 The FBI's latest additions to the JFK Collection at the National Archives, resulting from a Trump Presidential Executive Order in 2025, include well-known files. The latest versions of these records reveal the FBI's undue deference to the CIA in classifying its own records on surveillance inside the United States. Beginning in the 1960s, the FBI surrendered its domestic counterintelligence mandate to an agency

Two names of people who received copies are redacted under a national security exemption.[63] (See Appendix II.)

The FBI declined to declassify these memos in 2024 when I asked for them as part of my FOIA request for documents related to the Pellston plane crash. In an appeal to the Department of Justice, I was told I could file a new FOIA request for them or take the Bureau to court.

On April 30, 1970, President Nixon authorized an invasion of Cambodia, expanding a war he had promised to end. The decision was met with widespread protest. On May 4, 1970, when Ohio national guardsmen fired on them, four student protesters at Kent State University were killed and nine wounded. In the following days, student strikes and protests shut down 450 colleges and universities. When he heard about the students killed at Kent State, Walter sent a telegram to the White House:

> Your decision to invade the territory of Cambodia can only increase the enormity of the tragedy.... Widening the war merely reinforces the bankruptcy of our policy of force and violence in Vietnam....The bitter fruits of this growing alienation and frustration among America's youth are now being harvested on the campus of Kent State University....It is your responsibility to lead us out of the Southeast Asian war to peace at home and abroad.[64]

supposedly responsible only for espionage outside U.S. borders. The handwritten notations "referred to another United States Government agency" are found on fully declassified and newly located documents. That agency was the CIA. Nagle, Chad. "From the JFK Files: FBI Ceded Domestic Intelligence Operations to CIA," *JFK Facts*, April 21, 2025.

63 Ibid.

64 Elisabeth Reuther Dickmeyer, *Putting the World Together My Father Walter Reuther: The Liberal Warrior*, LivingForce Publishing, 2004. P.344

Chapter 6. May 9, 1970

On Saturday evening, May 9, 1970, Walter and Oskar Stonorov agreed to visit the new education center on the shores of Black Lake in rural Michigan for a final inspection. A UAW convention had just voted to name the new facility the Walter P. Reuther Family Education Center. Walter's wife, May, and a bodyguard, William Wolfman, would accompany them.

The new Black Lake center was located 40 miles east of the Emmet County Airport, which was near the city of Pellston. The UAW had chartered a Learjet (N434EJ) to ferry the party to the airport. It was the identical model, an LJ-23, regularly used by Reuther, the same model that had the dangerous hard landing at Dulles Airport a year and a half before. The flight was scheduled for a 7:30 pm departure from Detroit Wayne County Airport. Stonorov's Philadelphia flight was delayed, so the other travelers waited at the airport for his arrival.

The Learjet had begun its day at its home base, Columbus (Ohio) Airport. There are no reliable times for the flight between Columbus and Detroit City Airport. N434EJ landed and refueled at Akron, then left that airport at an unknown time, carrying singer Glen Campbell to Detroit City Airport, arriving at 7:00 pm. It debarked Campbell and then made the eighteen-mile straight line trip to Detroit Wayne County Airport, reaching it in time for the scheduled 7:30 departure. When Stonorov finally arrived, the group boarded the jet and the craft departed Detroit at 8:38 pm.

The Emmet County Airport in Pellston, Michigan, opened in May of 1936. By May of 1970, Emmet County Airport had two paved runways with four separate approach areas. One runway ran southwest to northeast, 5-23, with the southwest end known as Runway 5 and the northeast end known as Runway 23 (All airport runways have numbers corresponding to the runway's compass alignment—Runway 5 has a 50-degree reading). The approach end of Runway 5 had surrounding terrain as much as 300 feet higher within a quarter mile of the approach. Runway 14-32, running from the southeast to the northwest, was the primary runway at the airport and handled 82% of the air traffic.

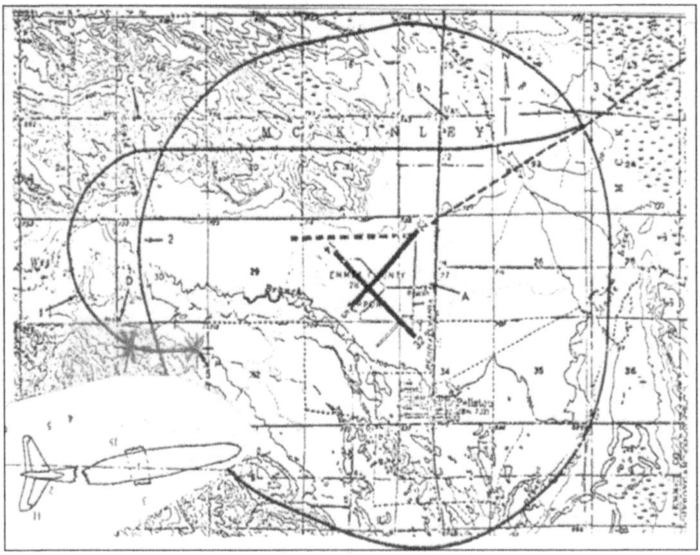

Map of the Pellston, MI airport, May 9, 1970, and the final flight path of ***N434EJ*****.**

N434EJ was under the control of the Minneapolis Air Route Traffic Control Center. The craft's pilot, Evans, requested to make a hard left and then a hard right en route to avoid some inclement weather, and permission was given. Minneapolis terminated their radar tracking at 9:14 and advised Evans to contact Pellston by radio. At 20 miles from Pellston, Evans asked for the weather and was told there were scattered clouds at 400 feet. The cloud ceiling was 800 feet with a visibility of seven miles, thunderstorms and light rain, wind varying from 80 degrees to 120 degrees, and intensity varying from 5 to 15 knots. The Flight Station Service (FSS) specialist, Thomas Sorrick, the only person at the airport that evening, asked whether the flight would land straight in on Runway 23 or circle to Runway 5.[65] Evans advised he would decide upon arrival.

At 9:23, Evans reported a procedure turn inbound, a circling motion that would commence a turn to the west instead of making a direct incoming approach at the No. 23 runway. The only lighted runway was 5, and there was no option but to circle. At 9:28, Evans announced the runway was in sight, and he was circling for a landing. There was no one to answer this last radio message from Evans because Sorrick had stepped outside to watch the craft before it began to circle.[66] This was bizarre behavior. In a later civil suit, the Airport Manager, Clarence Tatro, testified he had never seen an FSS specialist, including Sorrick, leave his desk to go outside and watch a landing. Sorrick also turned on the Flight Service Station recorder before stepping outside.[67] Tatro later testified that the recorder was used only in emergencies and borderline emergencies. When Sorrick turned on the recorder, the flight was in no trouble.

When N434EJ completed its circling movement, it began a descent to Runway 5. The plane's first impact with the tree line left a path of tree damage 255 feet in length and 45 feet wide. Small parts of the aircraft, including the nose cone, were strewn on the ground under those trees. After the first impact, the plane continued airborne for 15 to 20 seconds (one-half mile or 3000 feet) before striking the trees again and crashing to the ground. The plane erupted into fire, and all the bodies were burned beyond recognition. The craft was nearly completely destroyed. One of the intact sections was the avionics components.

65 Sorrick was not deposed in the civil action against the airport.

66 *National Transportation Safety Board Aircraft Accident Report. Executive Jet Aviation Inc. Lear Jet L23A N434EJ Near Emmet County Airport Pellston, Mi May 9, 1970. State of Michigan for the Circuit Court of the County of Emmet, Irving J. Bluestone, Administrator with the Will Annexed of the Estate of May W. Reuther Civil Action No. 173-3 Deposition of Clarence Tatro.*

67 Ibid.

NTSB issued its final report on December 22, 1970, days before the Christmas holiday. It cited the cause of the accident to be:

> Pilot visual illusions produced by the lack of visual cues during circling approach over unlighted terrain at night to a runway not equipped with approach lights or other visual approach aids. These illusions made the pilot think he was higher than his true position and were made more acceptable to him because of a strong possibility of an erroneous altimeter [a device used to measure altitude] reading.[68]

Concerning the captain's altimeter, the report states:

> Examination of the altimeter revealed that some incorrect parts had been installed, some parts were missing, one part was installed upside down, and a ring jewel was installed off center. Such conditions undoubtedly caused excessive friction. A set screw, which holds the calibration arm in place, may not have been tightly set. If the screw were loose, the altimeter would have read high by 225 to 250 feet.
>
> The Board believes that while the evidence is not conclusive, the captain's altimeter was probably reading inaccurately.

The copy of the report that the NTSB sent me in my second FOIA request contains several pages that, in an undated section titled "ERRATUM", were amended to replace three pages in the original report of December 1970. The corrected report added duties for the co-pilot during a circling approach, specifying they should call out deviations from normal altitude.

The amended report appears on pages 40-43, which are hand-marked. It jumps from Appendix C, marked page 24, to these pages. The report appears to be missing sixteen pages, exactly the length of the Kollsman Instrument and Barfield Instrument Corporation's written reports on the altimeter.

68 Ibid.

Kollsman manufactured the altimeter, and Barfield did the first examination of it.[69]

The NTSB report does not explain why experienced pilot Evan chose not to use the direct approach landing on Runway 23 and instead circled the airfield and used Runway 5. It was a fatal decision. Runway 5 was the only approach path not equipped with Runway End Identifying Lights (REIL).

- These lights are placed on both ends of the runway and consist of a pair of synchronized flashing lights.

- They help pilots identify the runway's end and provide a quick visual reference during the approach.

At the Pellston Airport, there were two REILs, one on each side of every Runway except No. 5. They were placed 40 feet in front of the edge of the Runway. At some time, Runway 5 had been equipped with REILs, but they were removed and moved to Runway 32 in 1967, and on May 9, 1970, No. 5-23 had edge lights that ran along the sides of the runway. Edge lights are white and define the lateral boundaries of the runway.

The Airport: Deposition of Clarence Tatro

February 3, 1973

Clarence Tatro was the first person deposed in the *Civil Action of the Reuther Estate v. The County of Emmett.* The Reuther Estate attorney, Donald Shely, questioned him. His deposition is approximately 100 pages long.

Tatro was 58 and unemployed at the time of the deposition. He had lived in Pellston most of his life and had an 8th grade education. He had been a machinist in Detroit in the 1930s and, during the war, worked at Ford Willow Run as a foreman, then became a maintenance engineer for Michigan Bakeries. He took a job as an Assistant Airport Manager at the Pellston Airport in 1967. Tatro did general airport work, maintenance, and airplane

69 Ibid. Erratum is a Latin word for error. An erratum refers to correcting an error in a published text, such as a book, article, or report.

fueling. In early 1968, he became the Airport Manager, overseeing the whole operation of the airport.

In the deposition, Shely questions Tatro about the airport's lighting system. Tatro was responsible for the maintenance of the lighting system and did most of the work himself. Shely asks Tatro about a REIL light being burned out on Runway 23 on the night of May 9, 1970. Tatro says he was not told about this at the time. Sorrick, the FSS specialist at the airport that evening, was aware that the light was out but did not report it. The morning after the crash, Tatro learned from the FAA about the REIL being out on Runway 23 and investigated it. Tatro said, "I think I changed the tube in it or something of that nature." There were both bulbs and tubes in the REILs. Tatro also testified that REILS could malfunction due to a blown fuse in the transformer located at the airport. The FAA should have been informed about this outage, but it wasn't. Tatro explains it was his responsibility to notify the FAA that a REIL was out. Shely asks Tatro what would happen if a REIL went out at 2:00 a.m. Tatro answers that the FAA would release a NOTEM (notice to pilot). Pilot Evans was not informed about the REIL being out.

Evan's fatal decision to circle to land at Runway 5 became a subject of interest in Shely's questioning of Tatro. Tatro finally had an opportunity to speak with the FSS specialist Sorrick at about 11:00 pm the evening of the crash:

Q: Was there any discussion about the favored runway?

A: Not to my knowledge.

Q: Did you have any information as to what had been the favored runway at the time you discussed this matter with him?

A: Yes, but I don't know where I received it.

Q: What was your information?

A: That runway 5 was favored.

Q: It is quite important to me, sir, to ask you where you obtained that information.

A: I can't recall.

Q: Did you by any chance obtain it from Mr. Sorrick?

A: I could have.

Q: Well, if you in fact did, did he indicate whether he had advised the pilot that that was the favored runway?

Mr. Stroup (attorney for Emmet County Airport): I will object to the question on the ground that it is merely calling for speculation from the witness, who has already testified that he doesn't recall.

Mr. Shely: If he can't answer it he may say so, but if he can I would like his answer.

A: I can't. That is too far away for specific details

Q: Weren't you anxious to find out how it happened?

A: Yes, very much.

Q: Didn't you attempt to obtain information from Mr. Sorrick as to how it happened?

A: That is possible.

Q: And didn't you in fact obtain some information from Mr. Sorrick as to what he knew about the event at the time you talked with him?

A: It is possible he told me.

Q: Is it only possible, or did you in fact?

A: I can't recall.

Q: Mr. Sorrick seems to have some trouble with his recollection. In any event, you can't tell us whether or not Mr. Sorrick indicated to you that evening that he had advised the pilot that 5 was the favored runway; is that right?

A: No, I can't.[70]

The most viable explanation for why Evans began circling the airport without any recorded conversation with Sorrick or without being notified of the faulty REIL on Runway 23 is that only the Runway 5 portion of the lights were on. The NTSB accident report confirmed that during the approach of N434EJ only Runway 5 was lighted. Tatro tells Shely that the pilots requested what lights they wanted to be turned on before landing and normally not half the lights went on in one direction and the other half were off.

70 State of Michigan for the Circuit Court of the County of Emmet, Irving J. Bluestone, Administrator with the Will Annexed of Walter P. Reuther and Irving J. Bluestone, Administrator with the Will Annexed of the Estate of May W. Reuther Civil Action No. 173-3 Deposition of Clarence Tatro

Q: Was there any reason to your knowledge why 32 [the most heavily used runway with REILS] would not have been available for use?

A: No.

Q: How about 5?

A: Available

Q: And of course 23 was also?

A: Yes.....

Q: What were the circumstances which would bring the lights on?

A: Pilot request....

Q: When a pilot is landing, which runway lights are turned on? All of them—

A: Just the ones he requested....

Q: If you turned the runway lights on for 5-23, could you see them both for an approach to 23 and for an approach to 5?

A: You could.

Q: Not half the lights went on for one direction, and the other half for the other direction?

A: No. They all went on. You could land on either runway.

Journalist Michael Parenti investigated the crash in 1995 and wrote that pilot Evans attempted to land at the only lighted runway.[71]

Tatro attested that the NTSB had not questioned him about the runway lights. The only questions they asked him concerned the fire truck. After the plane crashed at 9:33, Sorrick did not call Tatro, the Airport Manager, but Gary Sobleski, an agent for North Central Airlines, a regional carrier. Sobleski called Tatro and told him an airplane had gone off the end of Runway 5. Tatro hurried to the airport and got the facility's fire truck, equipped with foam for aircraft fires. In his deposition, Tatro asks, "Why would anybody [Sorrick?] call a City Fire Department with nothing but water on it for an aircraft fire? You put water on kerosene, and it makes it worse."

Tatro and Sobleski arrived at the airport at about 9:45 pm. They searched the area southwest of the airport, believing that

71 Parenti and Norton, "The Wonderful Life and Strange Death of Walter Reuther," *Covert Action Quarterly*, 1995 No. 54, p.42

a plane had landed on Runway 23 and overshot it going off the end of Runway 5, as that is what Sobleski was told. They finally ended up at the crash site, but the local Sheriff told them it was all over and they weren't needed. Tatro explains, "I feel as though I could have saved more of the wreckage, and I could have kept the bodies from being burned as much as they were if I had been called properly." Tatro arrived at the airport proper at about 11:00 or 11:30 pm and engaged with Sorrick, testifying, "Well, I don't think he told me anything that happened. I think I kind of bawled him out a little bit, or something like that, for not notifying me first."

Some of the equipment at the airport, like the VOR, was the responsibility of the FAA. VOR stands for VHF Omni-directional Range. It's a radio navigation system used by aircraft for short-to-medium-range navigation. VORs provide pilots with a reliable means to determine their position and stay on course. The Pellston Airport VOR ran on commercial electric power, but if that failed, the FAA maintained a backup generator, which would automatically come on. During the deposition of Tatro, Shely queries, "Did you ever learn, sir, that the VOR had been alarming that evening? Did that information ever come to your attention?" Tatro: "No." An alarm goes off when the VOR malfunctions and goes off the air, another problem plaguing the Pellston airport that fateful evening.

The NTSB found that visual illusions at nighttime were a cause of the crash. When questioned about this, Tatro, a pilot himself, says, "Well, you have no visual reference on the ground to give you depth perception...you have to rely on your instruments." The instrument Evans had to rely on was his altimeter. Astonishingly, the captain's altimeter survived the smashup and resulting fire. When examined, it would show that the altimeter was reading over 200 feet too high at the time because of subtle defects. Parts of the critical information from the manufacturer's examination were omitted from the NTSB report, and the FBI, responsible for performing an investigation, failed to do one.

The Altimeter. Deposition of William B. Weston

July 24, 1973

William B. Weston, an investigator for the NTSB, was deposed in the *Civil Action of the Reuther Estate v. The County of Emmett* (Civil Action No. 173-3) beginning on July 24, 1973, in Washington D.C. The deposition concluded on July 26. He was also examined by the counsel for Plaintiff Stonorov (Oskar's wife Betty) in civil action numbers 71-1091, 72-784, 73-984, 73-985, and 73-986 for the Eastern District of Pennsylvania. Present during the three days of examination were attorneys for the Plaintiffs: the Reuther Estate, Stonorov, Wolfman and Defendants Executive Jet Aviation, Instruments and Flight Research, Col-Aire Inc. (the President of Col-Aire was in attendance), and Gates-Learjet Corp. Also in attendance were attorneys for the NTSB and the FAA. The Emmett County attorney did not make it under protest. The deposition is approximately 350 pages long.[72]

The Learjet Corporation manufactured the aircraft that was destroyed at the Pellston airport and Executive Jet Aviation leased it. According to the Executive Jet Aviation maintenance log, the altimeter was remanufactured by Instruments and Flight Research and overhauled by Col-Aire when it was found to be out of tolerance in September of 1969. A problem for the Plaintiffs here is that there is no evidence that the altimeter found at the crash site was the same one in the maintenance log. The evidence shows it was not the same one.

The NTSB interpreted rules to prohibit the giving of expert opinion testimony in civil suits for damages and read a statement on this. The parties reached some sort of stipulation off the record concerning this. Stonorov's counsel called Weston. Weston was an Air Safety Investigator for the NTSB. He worked

---

72 State of Michigan for the Circuit Court of the County of Emmet, Irving J. Bluestone, Administrator with the Will Annexed of Walter P. Reuther and Irving J. Bluestone, Administrator with the Will Annexed of the Estate of May W. Reuther Civil Action No. 173-3 Deposition of William B. Weston.

for United Airlines for 13 years as a systems specialist and had worked for the NTSB since 1967.

Weston was the System Group Chairman of the NTSB investigation of the May 9 crash. The investigation was divided among various groups. The crash happened at 9:33 pm on May 9. Traveling from the Washington D.C. area, Weston arrived at the site the following morning, May 10, at 11:00 am. An initial look at the path the plane cut through the treetops indicated that the N434EJ path was lower than desired. This suggested to Weston that it likely was an instrument misreading or an instrument faulty indication that caused the pilot to be lower than he thought. Weston then found the captain's altimeter in the destroyed cabin area. He pulled it out of the still-warm wreckage.

Weston also recovered the aircraft's pitot-static system, which is its plumbing system connecting the altimeter to outside air pressure and sent it to the FBI for testing. He received a report back from the FBI that said there was nothing suspicious about it. (In the course of two FOIA requests to the FBI on the Pellston incident, they never admitted to me that they had these records.)

Weston took the altimeter to Barfield Instrument Company in Miami, Florida, for examination. It was under his control the entire time. Before Barfield examined the altimeter, Weston took it to Pan American Airlines, where they could X-ray it as Barfield did not have the necessary equipment. Weston testified that the serial number on the captain's altimeter was S/N 078, but the serial number came from Executive Jet's maintenance records. No identification was visible on the altimeter.

Barfield and Kollsman Examination

The X-ray proved to be important. Barfield technicians cut into the altimeter with a hack saw and delicately peeled the case off. A brass screw was missing from the rocking shaft, and they found it in the case with aluminum deposits on it. At the time the X-rays were taken the screw was in the proper hole. The hole was aluminum and gave indications the threads were torn out. Barfield found the altimeter also had a loose end stone and a loose jewel in the movement. (I understand that the jewel is like those in watches.) There was also heat damage and some damage from impact. Barfield noted the observations and packaged it in plastic envelopes for Weston to take. Barfield identified it as a basic Kollsman Type 2206. Weston brought the altimeter back to his office in Washington, where it remained locked for a week at his desk.

Weston then took the altimeter to Kollsman Instruments in Elmhurst, New York, for further examination and testing on May 26 and 27. They took photos throughout the examination of the altimeter. Weston testified about what Kollsman found: "Concerning the condition of the set screw, it appeared that the threads in the hole were torn, and I think that's pretty visible on [photos] 24,25...there's deformation of the threads..." Shaft A has the missing ring stone in the rear of the shaft, photo 37. Shaft A to the capsule, is the link which had the improper link pin in the spring pin on the capsule....it would put an unnatural torque on the thing...it was a pin, but it was out of another altimeter.... The forward jewel for this shaft was damaged, photo 38....The forward endstone for Shaft B was put in the mechanism backwards....One of the pivots which supports the rear of the rocking shaft was incorrect in that it is intended for a ring stone application only."

Kollsman constructed an identical model with the same abnormalities and found, "If the questionable calibration arm set screws were loose at the time of approach under concern, the instrument would probably have indicated high by roughly 225 to 250 feet." In his deposition, Weston concurred with this. He attached the Kollsman findings to his final report to the NTSB Board.

Military Altimeter

In response to a question from Dillman, the FAA attorney, and with the agreement of the other attorneys, William Weston reads from the Kollsman report:

> No identification was present to trace the specific instrument. The mechanismic [*sic*] construction isolated the unit to one of three major types each of which had

> numerous variations none of which were TSO [Technical Standards Order a federal aviation regulation] certified. All of these types were essentially military.[73]

Inexplicably, none of this information made it into the NTSB Board's final report on the Pellston crash. The Board's report included the Kollsman test results showing that the altimeter was likely reading 225-250 feet too high, and they listed all the wrong, missing, misassembled, and damaged parts but not the summary. The report discusses the altimeter as if it is the one identified in Executive Jet's maintenance log, though Kollsman found no identifying marks. There is no discussion about how such a poorly manufactured altimeter, made for the military, came out of Col-Aire, the last organization to handle it according to the maintenance log, and could have functioned properly for six months. Weston had no evidence that Col-Aire had incorrectly assembled, repaired, or inspected the altimeter.

Sabotage

On the second day of testimony, while objecting, FAA attorney Dillman stated, "I'm representing the United States government, and to whatever extent that applies to the NTSB—I'm not prepared to state whether that includes the NTSB." The NTSB had its attorney present.

The following day, Dillman asked Weston if his group, the Systems Group, would specifically look for evidence of sabotage. Weston answered, "No, sir. I think that falls into the jurisdiction of the Federal Bureau of Investigation."

Q: May I assume then that when you had your organizational meeting and you discussed, to whatever you discussed, areas that you were going to concentrate on or set your priorities, that sabotage was not one of the items that you were primarily looking for or at any rate it was somewhere way down on the list of priorities?

73 State of Michigan for the Circuit Court of the County of Emmet, Irving J. Bluestone, Administrator with the Will Annexed of Walter P. Reuther and Irving J. Bluestone, Administrator with the Will Annexed of the Estate of May W. Reuther Civil Action No. 173-3 Deposition of William B. Weston.

A: We never rule out the possibility of sabotage. If we do—and I don't believe it was discussed at least by my group. I am sure there must have been an FBI man there and there always is in the case of a fire or crash. It's one of the considerations that is discussed by the investigator in charge.

Q: Was there an FBI agent?

A: I don't remember. I think there was, but I don't remember. (Discussion off the record.)

Q: Mr. Weston, with regard to what your counsel has just explained to us, did you say previously that FBI agents normally appear at NTSB investigations?

A: Yes.

Q: But you don't recall in this instance whether or not there was one or there wasn't?

A: Vaguely, I remember, but like I said, there's been a lot of accidents since then.

Q: Would an FBI agent's participation in this investigation or any investigation be independent of the Board's inquiry, or would he be considered part of the NTSB investigating team?

A: I believe he would be independent.

Mr. Paffel (NTSB attorney): Yes.

A: Yes.

Q: May I assume there probably would be no record in the NTSB docket, and probably no record in the files of the NTSB of an FBI agent?

A: That would be a good assumption.

The NTSB field investigators faced a dilemma investigating possible sabotage. This was an area reserved for the FBI. Weston sought other explanations for the anomalies in the altimeter. His testimony on the set screw is an example of this. The Kollsman Instrument report that he referenced had photos. Concerning the condition of the set screw hole, Weston says, "It appeared that the threads in the hole were torn, and I think that's pretty visible on [photos] 24, 25... There's deformation of the threads." Weston states, "It was caused by the heat." Kollsman tested a similar altimeter, heating it to 1100 degrees (F) for two hours. The set screw did not come loose, and the threads were not damaged.[74]

74 Kollsman Instrument Corporation report on the altimeter conducted on May 26 and 27, 1970. Those in attendance: Mr.

When asked about any other abnormal condition with the shaft besides the tearing of the threads, Weston replies, "On picture No. 24, there's an indentation, and at the time, we were worried as to whether that was some sort of an indentation caused by a drill bit or something, and in testing this other one, we found that the heat causes this metal to puck." In an answer to another attorney, Weston says: "Yes. I repeat, as I said a little earlier, there's a slight indentation which was rather curious in that it appeared to look like a drill had been started into the area."

Occam's Razor principle suggests that among competing hypotheses, the one relying on the fewest assumptions should be the most likely. I asked for the Kollsman report in a FOIA request with the NTSB in 2018, and they denied having it. Maverick journalist A.J. Weberman found the Kollsman report in 1992 at the NTSB archives in Washington D.C. (he shared a copy with me) and wrote that the most likely explanation was that a drill had been used on the altimeter. It made the indentation, and then when the bit was put in the set screw hole, it tore out the aluminum threads. The set screw was placed back in the hole (where it remained at the time it was X-rayed for Barfield). But on the flight to Pellston, the torque and friction from all the wrong and misassembled parts slowly began pulling it out, causing the altimeter to read 225-250 feet too high when the jet attempted to land.[75]

According to the Emmett County Court documents, this issue of the lawsuit was resolved amicably out of court on October 9, 1975, days before it was scheduled to go to trial. In 1975, Elisabeth Reuther received a settlement of $6,569 from the Pellston Airport.[76]

William Weston (NTSB), Ted Cymmer (FAA May 27 only), Mr. John Stanislaw (Executive Jet Inc), Mr. James Angus (Kollsman), Mr. Peter Redmond (Kollsman)

75 A.J. Weberman, "*Did Nixon Run A Domestic Operation Phoenix*? "Fatal "Accidents" During The Nixon *Administration*. https://educationforum.ipbhost.com/topic/15078-was-joe-biden-the-target-of-a-botched-assassination-attempt-by-cia%E2%80%99s-domestic-operation-phoenix-component/?tab=comments#comment-175317

76 Email from Bruce Dickmeyer 2024.

Chapter 7. The Cover-Up

The Michigan State Police advised the FBI at 3:40 am Sunday, May 10, that a chartered plane had crashed just south of Pellston, and they believed Walter Reuther to be one of the deceased. One hour and ten minutes later, at 4:50 am, in a memo marked urgent, the Detroit Office notified FBI Director Hoover of this. (See Appendix II.) Although there was no request for FBI assistance, three more memos were sent to Hoover that day. Detroit informed Hoover at 2:00 pm and 10:06 pm that no positive identification had been made of the bodies. Finally, at 11:03 pm, the FBI Director was told the body of Walter Reuther had been positively identified using dental records. Although an FBI investigation of a crash like this was routine, there is no record that one ever took place.[77]

Following Reuther's funeral, the UAW executive board met to begin the selection of a new president. The union's constitution provided that a majority vote of the International executive board would fill a vacancy. Walter had made it known he favored Fraser to replace him. According to Paul Schrade:

> I found out later what had happened was that, during GM negotiations, I believe, in '67, Leonard was either drunk or being outrageous in terms of a strategy

77 FOIPA Request No.: 1543705-000 (See Appendix II)

session with Walter present, Doug present, and Irving Bluestone present. And Walter at that point told Victor and a few others—I think Doug and probably May—that "That man can never be president of the union; he's just too unstable."[78]

Pellston crash site May 10, 1970.

78 UCLA Library Center for Oral History Research. Interview with Paul Schrade. Tape X Side Two

Secretary-Treasurer Emil Mazey announced he would privately consult with each board member, and his poll showed that Leonard Woodcock and Douglas Fraser were in a dead heat. The initial count was thirteen to twelve in favor of Fraser, but one regional director switched his vote to Woodcock, giving him a narrow majority. Emotions were running high as many board members felt close to each candidate.

Some staff became involved—including Victor Reuther, for one—and this left scars that never healed. Woodcock threatened to demand a special convention as the final arbiter to reconsider the board's decision if he lost by one or two votes. Unwilling to prolong the contest, Fraser withdrew. At a May 22 meeting, Woodcock was elected unanimously.[79]

Years later, Schrade and Victor spoke with Fraser about his decision to withdraw:

> After that, I said, "Doug, what happened in 1970?" I said, "I was suspicious that something was going on between you and Woodcock." He said, "You were right." So Victor said, "What?" And he said, "Yeah, one session I had with Leonard, he said, 'Look, Doug, you can win this thing. But I want you to know my intentions. If you do, I'm going to resign from the administration caucus, and I'm going to go out and campaign against you every day, every week, on into the next convention.'" So, Doug said, "At that point, I thought it was best for the union that I not run. I didn't want the union disrupted."[80]

Five days after Woodcock assumed the presidency, he was presented with a memo on the Pellston crash from the UAW General Counsel, Stephen Schlossberg. May 27, the date of Schlossberg's memo, is the same day Kollsman Instruments finished their examination and testing of the altimeter, finding it was likely reading 225-250 feet too high at the time of the crash and that it had been made for the military and had no identi-

79 Barnard, *American Vanguard*. P. 462-463

80 UCLA Library Center for Oral History Research. Interview with Paul Schrade. Tape X Side Two July 24, 1990

fying markings. No single action was more responsible than this memo for the failure to properly investigate Reuther's death at the time or in the decades since. It is filled with falsehoods, easily discernable misinformation, and complete fabrications. All the essential details presented as facts by Schlossberg would be contradicted by the NTSB's final report eight months later.

Schlossberg begins his report by telling Woodcock he had spent May 25 with Governor Reed (former Republican governor of Maine), the Chairman of the NTSB, its General Counsel, and the team chief investigating the Reuther accident. Reed was close to President Lyndon Johnson, who appointed him to the Transportation Safety Board in 1966.

John H. Reed's relationship with Lyndon B. Johnson was instrumental in shifting his career from state-level politics to federal government roles after he lost the 1966 election for governor of Maine. Reed was a strong supporter of the Vietnam War. The Johnson connection helped Reed establish himself in Washington, D.C., laying the groundwork for his continued service under multiple administrations. In 1976, President Gerald Ford appointed Reed as U.S. Ambassador to Sri Lanka and the Maldives.

Schlossberg tells Woodcock the immediate question he needs to answer is whether he wants the NTSB to have a public hearing concerning the accident. A factual report should be ready in ten days but an analysis of the cause of the accident could take a year to a year and one-half. (The NTSB report was out less than eight months later.) Schlossberg writes:

> My personal feeling as a result of our conference on Monday is that a public hearing would serve no useful purpose because oral testimony would seem to be of little relevance. However Governor Reed has agreed not to make a decision until I inform him of your wishes in the matter.[81]

81 I obtained a copy of Schlossberg's report from A.J. Weberman in 2023. It was in a group of papers he had received from David Norris. It is stamped with "Archives of Labor History and Urban Affairs University Archives Wayne State University"

Schlossberg's report moves into a timeline of the flight. The Learjet was initially assigned to a ferry job from Columbus to Akron. According to Schlossberg, the Learjet left Columbus at 17:52 (5:52 pm) and arrived in Akron at 17:56 (5:56 pm).[82] Schlossberg recounts that flying from Columbus to Akron took four minutes. This is the first indication that some of these times are nonsensical. The plane refueled at Akron-Canton Airport, and Glen Campbell, the folk singer, boarded.[83] It left for the Detroit City Airport at 19:35 (7:35), landing at 19:00 (7:00 pm). The report says the flight arrived in Detroit 35 minutes before it left Akron. The two cities are in the same time zone.

None of the times noted in the Schlossberg memo should be uncritically accepted as accurate. According to Schlossberg, after debarking Campbell, the Learjet flew to the Wayne County Metro Airport "immediately" and was only on the ground there for twenty minutes, including taxiing in and out, before it loaded Walter and his party and departed at 20:44 (8:44). The arrival time at Detroit City Airport may be accurate. The NTSB report said the flight was scheduled to leave Detroit Metro at 19:30 (7:30). It is only eighteen straight-line miles between the two Detroit airports, which would have put the jet at Wayne County Metro between 7:15 and 7:25, in time for the scheduled departure at 7:30. Schlossberg says they left at 20:44 (8:44), and the NTSB said 20:38 (8:38). This is not twenty minutes but one hour and twenty minutes. The Pellston flight left late because Stonorov's flight from Philadelphia was delayed. Twenty minutes was not enough time to install a sabotaged altimeter; but one hour and twenty minutes is.

Replacing an altimeter in a Learjet Model 23 during the 1970s would have been relatively straightforward for an experienced avionics technician, provided he had access to the correct replacement parts, tools, and equipment. When an altimeter is replaced or recalibrated, it may take several minutes. The Learjet 23, a light business jet, typically had mechanical or electromechanical altimeters that required connections to the aircraft's

82 All times are eastern standard time in the 24-hour clock

83 Bill Gallagher, the Detroit TV reporter, told me he had interviewed Victor Reuther and Victor believed Campbell had been involved in the crash because of his right-wing politics.

static pressure system. Proper removal and reconnection of these fittings and electrical connections are necessary during this process. Before switching out an altimeter, the electrical system must be shut off to ensure safety, which can take about 1-2 minutes. The altimeter is located in the cockpit panel. For the physical replacement, a mechanic or pilot could remove the old unit and install the new one in the same position. This requires removing the mounting screws, securing the new altimeter to the instrument panel, and ensuring proper alignment. Then, secure the new altimeter with the mounting screws and reconnect the static system lines to the new altimeter.

This task would likely take about 5 to 10 minutes, depending on how accessible the instrument is. The Learjet Model 23's instrument panel was designed with ease of access in mind, but removing and reinstalling the altimeter still required care to avoid damaging neighboring instruments. Based on general aviation maintenance practices and the typical procedure for instrument replacement in light jets of that era, the complete process of switching and calibrating an altimeter in a Learjet 23 could take between 15 and 30 minutes. Clearly, no calibration would have been performed in this case. Thus, the job could have been completed in just a few minutes. All the witnesses to what happened to the Learjet at the Wayne County Airport would be dead within a few hours.

Schlossberg lived in Detroit, flew regularly, and had to know that these times were not truthful. Both his description of the jet leaving Detroit City Airport "immediately" and writing that the plane was only on the ground for "twenty minutes" at Detroit County Metro seem intended to discount any possibility of sabotage. This timeline did incalculable damage. Although Victor Reuther believed Walter had been assassinated and stated so publicly, he used Schlossberg as a source for the time on the ground at Detroit in his autobiography, *The Brothers Reuther* (1976). I quoted Victor's account in my book *El Golpe: U.S. Labor the CIA and the Coup at Ford in Mexico* (2022).

Another critical factor in the smash-up was the landing attempt at Runway 5 instead of Runway 23. In its report, the NTSB offered no explanation for this decision. Schlossberg narrates a discussion that he alleges took place between the

Flight Station Service specialist and the pilot: "The flight service attendant told the pilot... that there would be a strong tailwind if he continued in on Runway 23. The pilot answered when questioned about his intentions that he would land into the wind rather than with a strong tailwind." This entire exchange was a complete fabrication. Sorrick recorded the final conversation with Evans for some reason, and this exchange was not on the tape. If Schlossberg did not know this was a lie when he wrote it, he would have learned that when the NTSB report was published in December. This is what the NTSB stated about the final conversation.

> The Flight Service Station (FSS) specialist requested whether the flight would land straight in on Runway 23 or circle for Runway 5. N434EJ advised that the decision would be made later. At 2123 [9:23], N434EJ reported procedure turn inbound and received from the FSS the same weather as previously received. At 2125 [9:25], the flight reported the VOR inbound and was told that the wind was from 80 degrees at 8 knots. At 2128 [9:28], N434EJ reported runway in sight and that it was circling for a landing. This was the last communication from N434EJ.[84]

In his report to Woodcock, Schlossberg lists several possible reasons for the crash, but none were the actual causes. Regarding the altimeter, he wrote, "Faulty Altimeter—this possibility is discounted because there were two altimeters in this particular Lear Jet, but the instrument is still being checked." The NTSB field investigator, Weston, determined the crash resulted from an altimeter problem during his first few minutes at the site and believed the altimeter was a likely cause of the accident. There were two altimeters on N434EJ, but in the circling approach, the NTSB affirmed, the co-pilot likely would have been looking to the left, and if he looked at an altimeter at all, he would have looked at the captain's.[85]

84 *National Transportation Safety Board Aircraft Accident Report Executive Jet Aviation Inc. Lear Jet L23A N434EJ Near Emmet County Airport Pellston, Mi May 9, 1970*, p. 3
85 Ibid. p. 15

Schlossberg concluded:

> In view of the fact that almost no one outside of top officials at Executive Jet could have known the identity of the passengers and there was little, if any, chance of ground tampering of the airplane, it appears to me that further investigation on a private basis is unwarranted. We have to look at this as a tragic accident and nothing more.[86]

Schlossberg argued that only trusted people could have known who was on N434EJ. Elisabeth, Walter's daughter, was skeptical of the official story, and she learned that a newspaper reporter knew her father was traveling to Black Lake nearly every weekend. As the UAW General Counsel, Schlossberg knew Walter's itinerary so he could be reached in emergencies. In an interview with A.J. Weberman, Victor Reuther said:

> I've had very strong suspicions from the day the accident occurred. I'm convinced there was tampering with the altimeter and although the plane was on the ground for only a short time, it was enough time. The full story was not told. When I wrote my book, I had not seen these files [Kollsman on the altimeter]. I relied on the then-General Counsel of the UAW, Steve Schlossberg, who I know from later experience was not too eager to make the investigation terribly thorough.... He was more interested in passing the reins of power to the new president, Leonard Woodcock, and getting the Reuther years behind him, so I felt he was too quick to accept the findings.[87]

Who was Stephen Schlossberg? Schlossberg came from an upper middle-class Jewish family from Roanoke, Virginia. His father immigrated from czarist Russia. He went to the University of Virginia, and when World War II started, he enlisted in the Army Air Corps and was in the military for five years and ten months. When he returned, he got a job as an organizer for the International Ladies Garment Worker Union (ILGWU). Unlike

86 Schlossberg's report to Woodcock

87 Weberman, "*Did Nixon Run A Domestic Operation Phoenix?*"

most ILGWU organizers, he spoke like a Southerner, successfully unionized workers, and was promoted to director of organizing for the Upper South. He worked for the ILGWU for five years.[88] In his work at the ILGWU, he would have interacted with David Dubinsky, the union's president and a staunch anti-communist often at odds with Reuther.

Schlossberg went on to the University of Virginia Law School, and after graduating, he went to a Washington, D.C., labor law firm. After several years there, he took a job with the Federal Mediation and Conciliation Service in 1961. In 1963, he was hired by the UAW as general counsel. After Reuther's death, Woodcock granted Schlossberg's request to be director of the Washington office. Still, he remained a general counsel and became a major player on the Washington political scene. His key goal at this time was to bring the UAW back into the AFL-CIO, which he achieved in 1979 when the Autoworkers rejoined the Federation.[89] In 1983, he left the UAW, joined a prestigious law firm, and practiced there until 1985 when William Brock, Republican President Ronald Reagan's Secretary of Labor, appointed him as Deputy Under Secretary of Labor. He headed the Bureau of Labor-Management Relations and Cooperative Programs. In 1987, Reagan appointed him to the United Nations position of director of the Washington office of the International Labor Organization. Schlossberg retired in 1994.[90]

In 1992 A.J. Weberman presented Schlossberg with the Kollsman file on the altimeter. Weberman wrote:

> Schlossberg was sent a copy of this analysis and contacted. He stated that as he understood it, the cause of the crash was a faulty altimeter. He took the technicians' word there was no evidence of sabotage. Steve Schlossberg told this researcher: "It's not my field. The technical part of the report was like a foreign language to me. I was impressed with the honesty of the people

88 Donald Smyth, *The Road Less Traveled; A Biographical Sketch of Stephen I. Schlossberg A Trade Union Life*, Peppertree Press, 2009, pp. 14-17

89 Interview with Stephen I. Schlossberg The Association for Diplomatic Studies and Training Foreign Affairs Oral History Project, Labor Series, Interviewed by: Morris Weisz, Initial interview date: June 25, 1993

90 Ibid. pp. 23-37

> who were doing this." He did not believe Walter Reuther's death was the result of a conspiracy, nor did he believe CIA had any motive to assassinate him. He elaborated: "Walter Reuther became a dove in the middle of the Hubert Humphrey–Nixon election. He was very much a hawk. A wonderful guy, but he was for the war. He was Johnson's biggest supporter. Walter finally opposed the war, but he never made it into a crusade. In the future, he probably would have, he was a wonderful guy, and it's too bad he didn't come around earlier. But when he did come around, it was great, and who knows what he would have developed into. Probably something wonderful."[91]

UAW president Leonard Woodcock decided not to support a public inquest into Walter Reuther's death, and none was held. The NTSB's final report, published eight months later, contained abundant detail about the Pellston catastrophe. Still, they omitted the information that the altimeter had been made for the military, had no identifying markings, and was not approved for use in civilian aviation. They did not address the issue of sabotage of the altimeter because that was the jurisdiction of the FBI, and the Bureau did not investigate the crash.

Between 2018 and 2021, I filed three FOIA requests with the NTSB for records concerning the Pellston crash. In the first one, I asked for the Kollsman Instrument report. They replied:

> In response to your FOIA request regarding an aviation accident on 05/09/1970 in Pellston, Michigan. The only information available is the final report on NTSB.GOV. Here is the web address to access the report.

The web link states that NTSB found the probable cause to be the pilot's inability to visually recognize how low the plane was because of the darkness and a faulty altimeter that was likely to have been reading 225–250 feet higher than the aircraft was.

Several years later, I presented the NTSB with a copy of the Board's final report from 1970, and they were able to locate a copy,

91 Weberman, "*Did Nixon Run a Domestic Operation Phoenix?*"

the same as the one I had given them, except it contained an additional cover page and several pages that, in an undated section titled "ERRATUM," were amended to replace three pages in the original report of December 1970. I filed another request asking for correspondence with the FBI concerning the crash and got this answer as part of a letter: "Therefore, other than the brief of accident report, available at this link: DCA70AZ008 (ntsb.gov), and the published aircraft accident report, AAR-71-03.pdf (ntsb.gov), there are no other records responsive to your request."

The NTSB did not respond to two emails asking for comment on the Kollsman report found in their archives in 1992 and Weston's testimony about it in the Reuther Estate civil suit.

Walter Reuther, president of the United Auto Workers union, addresses an audience at the UAW West Side Local 174, Detroit, Michigan. Behind him is the Federal Art Project / Works Progress Administration mural by the artist Walter Speck.

Chapter 8. The Suspects

Fifty years after a murder, it is difficult to determine which organizations and individuals were responsible. The most anyone can do today is examine motives, means, and opportunity. In 1992, a meeting occurred that would add a new dimension to concerns about the air crash that killed Walter Reuther. David O. Norris, a Licensed Private Detective, attended the Labor Museum and Learning Center opening in Flint that year. He was there with his friend, singer/songwriter Dan Hall, who was performing their song *1937 (When Spirits Burned)*. Norris was coauthor of the lyrics to the song, which had become a labor anthem.

David Norris was born and raised in Flint, Michigan. His father, Donald F. Norris, served as the director of Labor Relations for the Fisher Body Plant #1 in Flint. The elder Norris developed friendships with some of his counterparts in the UAW. He admired Walter Reuther, whom he held in high regard compared to what he perceived as dubious and bombastic union leaders of his time. David grew up in this auto industry environment and the traditions of Flint, where the UAW was founded during the sit-down strikes. He began his career as a country music disc jockey at a major radio station, where he worked in music production and also became interested in recording, and songwriting. David later became the Administrative Assistant to the mayor of Burton, MI. He also served as a police officer in Burton and was a Genesee County Deputy Sheriff before establishing his private detective agency, specializing in felony and homicide defense.

During a performance at the Labor Museum, Norris met Elisabeth Reuther Dickmeyer and her husband, Bruce Dickmeyer. It was during this time that David, Elisabeth, and Bruce discussed the plane crash that took the lives of her parents. Norris's natural curiosity as an investigator was piqued as he listened to Elisabeth's confusion about how little was known regarding the crash and the investigation—or the lack thereof. She was convinced that the plane crash was not an accident. Although she could never justify this belief, she knew her father always considered the possibility of assassination, as attempts had been made on both him and Victor. She noted that Walter believed he could unite the Old Left he represented with the New Left, the rising anti-war progressive left mobilizing in the streets.

At some point, Norris decided to inquire about what information remained. Although he never opened a formal file on the case, he felt he was working on behalf of Elisabeth and her husband for their peace of mind. From the beginning, Norris realized that the federal government was not forthcoming with information. He found it curious that when he requested the report on the plane crash, he was told it no longer existed and that only a brief descriptive account remained, which was sent to him. It amounted to about two paragraphs. When he later suspected that more information existed, he contacted then-Congressman Dale Kildee, who made a direct request to the FAA. Kildee received a several-page report regarding the plane crash—much more detailed than the few paragraphs he originally got. However, it still lacked the type of useful information that would allow him to continue a formal investigation. Later, while reading about some documents in the Emmett County Court file regarding the crash, he learned that some objects had been sent to the FBI crime lab for examination. This detail was not mentioned in the multi-page report supplied through Congressman Kildee's office. A brief inquiry with the FBI indicated that they had not investigated the crash, which seemed suspicious to Norris.

Norris theorized, certainly without any background in aviation, that the instruments controlling airspeed, particularly the pitot-static tube located on the leading edge of the wing or on the aircraft's body facing forward, could have been easily and quickly tampered with. This might result in a faulty airspeed reading and lead to a plane losing altitude. Norris never found an expert who could confirm whether enlarging a hole would increase static pressure in the pitot-static line, and aside from expressions like "it could..." or "that's possible," nobody dared to speculate.

The whole question of whether any conspiracy could have been involved in the fatal crash was dismissed by the note and conclusion Stephen Schlosberg sent to Woodcock in the days after the crash, stating that Executive Jet management insisted it was "impossible" for anyone other than trusted company officials to have known who would use the plane at the time of the flight, thus undermining any theory of a plot against Reuther. Norris believed it was nonsense to think that if there were any conspiracy related to the crash, it would easily be determined who might be aboard that Lear Jet. And yet, just hours after the crash, a *Detroit News* reporter spoke to the night dispatcher at Butler Aviation, who said he knew that Reuther, his wife, and a "bald-headed man" were on the plane. He recognized Reuther from previous flights. Norris thought that the dispatcher likely wasn't referring to a manifest if he didn't know that the "bald-headed man" was Oskar Stonorov. Elisabeth informed Norris that during that time, her father was flying up to Black Lake almost every weekend. It was a regular occurrence, and that information wouldn't have been hard to find.

During Norris's brief inquiry, neither he nor the Dickmeyers had the resources to consult experts or cover the expenses of pursuing FOIA and document requests through the FBI or FAA. If you can even call it that, the investigation faded into little more than ongoing friendly conversations and speculation between Norris and the Dickmeyers.

When asked about a motive for the assassination of Walter in 1995, Victor said, "Also I had exposed some CIA elements inside labor, and this was also associated with Walter. Although Walter knew I was right, he felt that I had put him in an impossible position. He said, 'You're taking on an agency that can forge any document to prove we are liars.'"[92]

For a decade, the Reuthers had been in conflict with the senior foreign policy leadership of the AFL-CIO and the CIA (it is difficult to determine where one began and the other ended). 1966, Victor publicly exposed their collaboration in the American Institute for Free Labor Development. In his interview with the *LA Times*, he called the AFL-CIO's foreign policy "a vest pocket operation run by Jay Lovestone." The AFL-CIO responded with a motion condemning Victor, which led to the UAW withdrawing from the Federation and creating a rival labor organization. In February 1967, in an interview with the *New York Post*, Victor asserted that the Agency had been involved in U.S. union elections. He said, "I did my best to try and lift the lid on it. And someday, it will all come out." Walter Reuther posed a threat to the CIA's ongoing operations around the world.

For twenty years before James Angleton, the CIA chief of counterintelligence, recruited him as an agent, Jay Lovestone was a mortal enemy of the Reuthers.[93] Angleton developed a close personal relationship with Lovestone, who became a virtual member of Angleton's family. They communicated almost every day for 20 years. Angleton was one of the more sinister figures to emerge during the Cold War. Among Angleton's noteworthy activities were Operation CHAOS and HT/LINGUAL. HT/LINGUAL was a CIA program that intercepted the mail of American citizens, opened it, copied it, and then sent it on. It was in effect from 1955 to 1973. During that time, agents opened 215,000 pieces of mail. One of those whose mail was intercepted was Victor Reuther. In 1967, Angleton began Operation CHAOS in response to the anti-Vietnam War movement. During the six years of its existence, it spied on 300,000 individual Americans and over 100 organizations opposed to the war in Vietnam. The CIA sent 5,000 reports to the FBI. Both programs were illegal. Angleton became obsessed with the idea

92 Parenti and Norton, "The Wonderful Life and Strange Death of Walter Reuther," Covert Action Quarterly, 1995 No. 54 p. 43.

93 In an email, Walter's son-in-law Bruce Dickmeyer wrote me, "Uncle Victor was also quite sure it wasn't an accident. And Victor thought the CIA was quite possibly involved. I remember him bringing up the names of Lovestone and Schlossberg."

that a Soviet mole had penetrated the Agency in 1960. In pursuit of the effort to uncover this phantom individual, Angleton and his office tracked Lee Harvey Oswald, Kennedy's accused killer, for four years before the JFK assassination. Angleton supervised Oswald's CIA file from October 1959 to November 1963. He was involved in covering up this and other CIA connections to the Kennedy assassination events for the rest of his life.[94] Angleton rises to the level of a suspect in Reuther's death.

The incredible complexity of developing an altimeter that would begin a flight working correctly but start reading too high shortly after take-off has convinced some that Reuther's death was not an assassination. In the CIA's declassified electronic reading room, a search of documents containing the word "altimeter" returns over 150 items. While most of these concern topics like high-altitude spy planes or Soviet military aircraft capabilities, the Agency was very familiar with altimeters. Of interest is one document labeled "Air America Inc. Vientiane, Laos, Facilities and Capabilities." Air America was a CIA-operated airline. The document, written in March 1973, details the size of the Laotian facility, 1,615 employees, and explains they operate a fleet of 58 aircraft. They could completely disassemble, inspect, and overhaul those aircraft. The Avionics Shop could refurbish and test most electronic equipment in the plane, including altimeters, and those were tested, repaired, and maintained regularly.[95]

The CIA operated a secret airbase within the U.S. Area 51, situated at Groom Lake in southern Nevada, was initially selected by the CIA in 1955 as a testing site for the Lockheed U-2, a high-altitude reconnaissance aircraft, under the code name Project AQUATONE. The site was chosen for its remote location, which facilitated safe and discreet testing of the U-2 and later other aircraft, such as the A-12 OXCART and the F-117 Nighthawk stealth fighter. The CIA, the U.S. Air Force, and defense contractor Lockheed Martin collaborated on these

94 Jefferson Morley, *The Ghost. The Secret Life of CIA Spymaster James Jesus Angleton*. St. Martin's Press, First Edition (2017), pp.56, 87, 188, 218, 219.
95 Central Intelligence Agency, "1973-03-07. "Air America, Inc. Vientiane, Laos Facilities and Operations," 197307 pdf. General CIA Records. Freedom of Information Act. Electronic Reading Room

projects at Area 51. The existence of Area 51 remained unacknowledged by the U.S. government until 2013, when declassified documents were released confirming its role in testing these reconnaissance aircraft. Despite this acknowledgment, many details about current and past activities, including black operations at Area 51, remain classified. It would have been well within the CIA's capabilities to assemble an altimeter that would inaccurately read altitude.[96]

In addition to an altimeter, an assassination would require an expert in commercial aviation and airports, Learjets, weather conditions affecting landings, altimeters, and willing to kill innocent people for political objectives. There is someone who might have fit that description. There is no evidence linking John Lear, Learjet founder Bill Lear's son, to the Reuther assassination. But he is a person of interest. Some regarded John Lear as the greatest commercial pilot in history. He held 17 world speed records and was the only pilot to hold every airman certificate issued by the FAA. He held the record for flying around the world, done in a Learjet that covered 22,000 miles in 50 hours and 39 minutes.

By his own account, John Lear worked for the CIA between 1967 and 1983.[97] At the time of Reuther's death, he wrote, he was in California either working for his own company that went bankrupt or for Learjet as a test pilot. His father fired him from his test pilot job, and they had a falling out. Gates-Learjet Corporation was a participant in the legal actions concerning the Pellston crash. A Learjet attorney was present at the 1973 deposition of NTSB field agent William Weston, who testified that the altimeter was reading over 200 feet too high at the time of the crash; it had been manufactured for the military, had no identification marks, and was not approved for use in civilian aviation. Learjet used Kollsman Instrument altimeters in its

96 Jacobsen, Annie. *AREA 51: An Uncensored History of America's Top Secret Military Base* Little, Brown and Company 2012. pp.69-80 pp. 419-427

97 United States District Court Southern District Of New York Dr. Morgan N. Reynolds, on behalf of The United States of America Plaintiff, vs. Science Applications International Corp. et al. Defendants. State of Nevada: County of Clark Affidavit ECF Case 07 CIV 4612 (GBD) January 28, 2008

planes and could have had access to the Kollsman report on the Pellston altimeter in 1970. It is likely Bill Lear and the others involved in the civil suit knew this had been an assassination. Bill Lear excluded John from his will but was generous with John's children. If Bill Lear learned that John had been involved in the Reuther assassination, might he have disinherited his son?

John Lear married for the second time in 1970 but soon left the country. In 1973, he was a pilot at a CIA airbase in Vientiane, Laos, supporting General Vang Pao's CIA-backed Hmong troops. This was the same CIA base referenced earlier in connection with the altimeter.

John Lear was involved in right-wing politics. He was a significant figure in what has been referred to as the "dark side movement," which is associated with conspiracy theories aligned with the far-right end of the political spectrum. This movement, led by Lear and others, believed in a ruthless "secret government" controlling the world and collaborating with alien races for advanced technology. Lear and his associates propagated these beliefs and theories intertwined with extremist political literature and flying-saucer folklore.[98]

John Lear became a prominent figure in UFO conspiracy theories in the 1980s. While he didn't originate the Area 51 conspiracy, he significantly contributed to its expansion and popularization. In March 1989, Lear introduced journalist George Knapp to Bob Lazar, a key figure in Area 51 lore. Lazar claimed to have worked on reverse-engineering alien technology at a site called S-4 near Area 51. This introduction brought significant attention to Area 51 and cemented its place in UFO conspiracy theories.

Lear, Gene Huff, and others claimed to have observed strange, glowing objects taking off from Groom Mountain near Area 51. These alleged sightings added credibility to the conspiracy theories surrounding the base. In December 1987, Lear released a statement on ParaNet, an early paranormal bulletin board, claiming that the U.S. government had secret contacts with extraterrestrials. His revised statement in 1988 detailed alleged

98 "John Lear and the Dark Side." The Editors of Publications International, Ltd. Updated: Apr 16, 2024. https://science.howstuffworks.com/space/aliens-ufos/john-lear.htm

treaties between a secret government committee (Majestic 12) and Gray aliens.[99]

In 1989, Lear served as "State Director" for MUFON (Mutual UFO Network), hosting the 1989 symposium "The UFO Cover-Up: A Government Conspiracy?" Despite initial objections from MUFON founder Walt Andrus, Lear was able to submit a slate of speakers after he threatened to split the symposium. At that same symposium, *The Roswell Incident* (1980) author Bill Moore tearfully confessed to having intentionally spread disinformation to UFO researcher Paul Bennewitz on behalf of purported counter-intelligence agent Richard Doty. One of their goals, Moore said, was to disseminate information and watch as it was passed from person to person in order to study information channels. Lear's speakers were slated to provide allegedly independent verification of the Bennewitz claims. One of those speakers, Bill Cooper, would later break with Lear after accusing him of being an intelligence agent. Lear promoted alleged UFO whistle-blower Bob Lazar and his tales of Area 51.[100]

Lear had the skill set that made him capable of planning and organizing the assassination of Reuther. He died in 2022.

The 8,400 pages of documents the FBI collected on Walter Reuther during the tenure of Director J. Edgar Hoover are a testament to Hoover's obsession with Reuther. The Bureau admitted to Bill Gallagher that they had 59 pages dated from 1967 to 1970. They released 38 of those to Gallagher, but seventeen were withheld because they were referred to another government agency. Four were withheld on national security exemptions. The released documents are heavily redacted. They show that information about Reuther was shared with the FBI's COINTELLPRO and Internal Security Section and externally with the Secret Service and G-2 (Military Intelligence). None of these organizations had anything to do with protecting Reuther.

Military Intelligence reportedly worked with the CIA in a top-secret organization called Field Operation Intelligence. It began

99 "Famed aviator John Lear, 79, departs on 'his next adventure'" George Knapp April 1, 2022 https://www.8newsnow.com/investigators/famed-aviator-john-lear-79-departs-on-his-next-adventure/

100 https://en.wikipedia.org/wiki/John_Lear

in the post-war Far East under General Charles Willoughby, who had overseen Military Intelligence in East Asia. Charles Andrew Willoughby was a major general in the U.S. Army who served as General Douglas MacArthur's chief of military intelligence (G-2) during World War II and the Korean War. In correspondence with CIA Director Allen Dulles, Willoughby said he created a new organization in which the CIA had autonomy but coordinated covert operations with the military. That apparently marked the beginning of FOI. After retiring from the U.S. Army in 1951, Willoughby became involved in publishing a newspaper called the *Foreign Intelligence Digest*. He worked with Texas oil tycoon L. Hunt on the International Committee for the Defense of Christian Culture, an extreme right organization that had connections to anti-communist groups, and was the organization's national executive secretary for a time.[101] A former government intelligence agent, Richard Case Nagell, claimed he worked for the FOI inside the U.S. during the 1960s.[102] When copies of the background check on the individual with a "contract" on Reuther were sent to G-2 in 1969, they may have also reached the CIA.

101 David A. Foy, (2023). *Loyalty First: The Life and Times of Charles A. Willoughby, MacArthur's Chief Intelligence Officer*. Havertown, Pennsylvania: Casemate Publishers pp. 206-207.

102 Dick Russell, *The Man Who Knew Too Much.* Carroll & Graf Publishers, 1992, pp. 50-51, 68

Chapter 9. Postmortem

Weeks after assuming office, Woodcock faced the expirations of the Big Three auto contracts. In 1967, the UAW was forced to agree to a cap on the COLA with the Big Three, resulting in widespread discontent in the union and demands to reinstate it. GM had not been targeted as the pattern setter in the last five rounds of negotiations. The GM membership was militant and ready for a fight. Consensus about confronting the largest employer in the U.S. developed, and Woodcock could not look weak or show a lack of resolve. The UAW began a strike on September 14, 1970. It became long, painful, and difficult.

Woodcock had worked with Reuther for many years, but he conducted negotiations differently. There were fewer tactical innovations, less creativity, and fewer emotional outbursts with more rational analysis and sober argument. One of the disadvantages of striking GM was that the union was ill-prepared to financially support such a massive work stoppage. Many UAW staff were laid off and the rest of the officers and staff took a 50% pay cut.[103] The Teamsters union gave the UAW a loan, and GM agreed to continue paying health care premiums even though they were under no contractual obligation to do so. This was leverage for GM during the conflict. Woodcock entered private negotiations

103 Barnard, *American Vanguard*. PP. 468-476

with the GM CEO to end the strike in an unprecedented move. The COLA cap was removed, but other demands weren't met. Over some opposition, the GM council, comprised of local union officers, approved the tentative agreement, and the members overwhelmingly ratified it. Region director Schrade recalled:

> I had some problems with the negotiation and Woodcock's performance, too, because he seemed always too respectful of the power of GM and the top executives. When the final deal was made on the strike, it was Woodcock going alone, as he said, "up to the fourteenth floor" of the GM building to meet with the top guy where it was agreed that things had to be worked out and they would settle the strike. And that kind of solo negotiations Reuther never would have done.... To me, it was not the Reuther style of militant bargaining and very careful recognition of the rights of the national committee of local union representatives and the membership. It was more autocratic than Reuther was, who was considered an autocrat anyway, but at least he was very conscious of the need for maintaining the trust and confidence of the rank and file in the national committee, and I could not see Woodcock doing this. He had a whole different style which I objected to and still do.[104]

Woodcock had surreptitiously worked to defeat Schrade as Region director at the 1970 constitutional convention before Walter's death, but as President, he could now move more decisively to oust Schrade. He supported a local leader who was more pro-war than Schrade. Woodcock viewed Schrade as an opponent on the IEB. When Schrade lost the 1972 election for Region Director, he returned to his old Rockwell Corporation job. Schrade considered Reuther his mentor for many years, and among other notable assignments in his career, Reuther sent him to establish contacts with the Farmworkers Union and Cesar Chavez. He would later say:

104 UCLA Library Center for Oral History Research. Interview with Paul Schrade. Tape X, Side Two, July 24, 1990

> I was really hurt by it, but then again the kind of union we were going to have with Woodcock was not the kind of union that I wanted, because he was much more conservative than Fraser and that began coming out, whereas we had really very progressive leadership from Walter most of the time, except on the war. The character of the union changed, and Leonard was very difficult to deal with on a personal basis much of the time.[105]

The Woodcock years marked a break with Walter Reuther's social unionism. Some of this was due to differences in leadership, but much of it was caused by sweeping changes in the world economy. Globalization was the major source of change that would alter the UAW, the United States, and the rest of the world.

In the 1980s, the Big Three automakers began fundamentally restructuring their operations. This transformation was forced by two oil crises and the resulting increase in demand for small fuel-efficient vehicles, more stringent regulations on safety, energy, and the environment in the U.S., and a drastic fall in vehicle demand overall. Japanese automakers were able to take advantage of the changing competitive dynamics by using new technologies and production methods, like lean production and just-in-time delivery. They also held a competitive cost advantage over American operations.

During the U.S. military occupation of Japan following World War II, occupation forces initially encouraged unions as a democratic element of society that could counteract re-militarization. Amid the poverty and hardship of early post-war Japan, unions flourished. They contested with employers as both struggled to adapt to the new rules and the increasing power afforded to workers. As the Cold War intensified, the U.S. backed purges of communists who had gained influence in the new Japanese unions and began to limit support for unionization. In the spring of 1953, a conflict erupted between Japan's strongest auto union and Nissan (supported by the Bank of Japan and the government), ultimately leading to the reshaping of the auto industry worldwide.

105 Ibid.

On May 25, 1953, a 100-day strike and lockout began at the Nissan plant, involving 7,000 union members. Unlike in the U.S., middle management employees were permitted to join the union in Japan. A new union, supported and financed by Nissan management, was created to oppose the striking union. This new union, led by members of management, competed with the old union for membership. Fistfights between the factions occurred regularly. The non-communist leftist leader of the striking union was arrested and jailed after rushing a company barricade. By early September, Nissan broke the strike and defeated the old union, which was replaced by a new company union that became the workers' representative. The production methods that would later dominate manufacturing worldwide emerged from this new union-management relationship: lean manufacturing.[106]

The new production system was initially called just-in-time production. It was further refined as the Toyota Production System, then came to be called lean manufacturing. Lean manufacturing is a method that focuses on minimizing waste while maximizing productivity. The system requires a high degree of cooperation from the workforce, and if a union represents those workers, it requires a collective bargaining agreement that allows employers the necessary degree of flexibility.

Beginning in the 1970s, the UAW-represented auto manufacturers were losing market share and profits to the Japanese and German imports. A parade of foreign-owned companies built factories in rural small-town areas in Ohio, Kentucky, Tennessee, South Carolina, and Alabama, where the people lacked interest in and support for labor unions. These companies proved to be almost impossible for the UAW to organize. They drew on a Japanese workplace culture that emphasized the common interests of workers and managers and presented the employers as caring parents.[107] This worked well with the paternalistic industrial code of the U.S. South.

106 David Halberstam, *The Reckoning*. A Thomas Congdon Book, First Edition (1986), pp. 111–187.

107 I traveled to Japan as part of a four-member UAW delegation as guests of the Japanese Institute for Labor in the summer of 1999 to study the Japanese auto industry and culture.

The Detroit Big Three employers responded to these developments in two ways: by moving some production to the extremely low-wage country of Mexico and by launching their versions of cooperative programs, which the UAW adopted. Irving Bluestone was the principal UAW champion of "quality circles," "quality of worklife," and "employee involvement." These programs eventually morphed into full replicas of the Toyota Production System and lean production, transforming the UAW. Paul Schrade clearly described the union political ramifications of the changes:

> And one of the things that has happened that I think is most abhorrent in the jointness thing and this cooperative effort with the corporations is that there's a whole new cadre of union members working within the system who are now part of the managerial system. And they are paid by the corporation and generally appointed by both the union and the corporation. They have to be acceptable to the corporation. They now serve as a political arm of the administration of the union, and since they don't want their jobs eliminated by the people who oppose the team concept of jointness, hundreds of these people are now within the corporation who are out campaigning against any oppositionist to this kind of policy. So, the union leadership now has an unfair advantage in terms of the politics of the union.[108]

How would Walter Reuther have dealt with wide-ranging changes in the world economy? As a man who spent many years of his youth living and working abroad and who held strong positions on international worker solidarity, he would likely have been better positioned to address those problems than his successors, who responded with feeble, ineffective "Buy America" programs and concessions.

Reuther had expressed skepticism about putting union people into management-type positions in the workplace. It is difficult to picture him becoming an advocate for permanently

108 UCLA Library Center for Oral History Research. Interview with Paul Schrade. Tape XI Side One July 24, 1990

institutionalized cooperation with the auto companies. Victor Reuther's alliance with Jerry Tucker and the New Directions Movement, which was highly critical of the new joint programs, says much about how Walter would have viewed the new spirit of strategic cooperation with the auto companies.

A troubling question about Reuther's assassination concerns the UAW leadership. Irving Bluestone, a UAW vice president and reputedly the closest officer to Reuther, was the administrator of the estate of Walter Reuther and May Reuther. The estate hired Donald Shely from the Detroit law firm of Dykema, Gossett, Spencer, Goodnow, and Trigg for the civil action against Emmet County. Shely did an admirable job in the deposition of airport manager Clarence Tatro. Shely focused on the crash in a manner that demonstrated he knew that what had transpired had been an assassination. He aggressively questioned Tatro about the runway light that was out on runway 23 and why the FAA had not been notified. He focused on why the Learjet was diverted to runway 5, forcing the pilot to rely on his altimeter. Shely asked about the strange behavior of the Flight Service Station specialist Sorrick, whom he had questioned off record. When he learned that Tatro had been given the wrong location of the crash site, he explored the consequences of not getting the emergency fire truck there promptly. The Reuther estate attorney had researched events and told Tatro that the VOR had been malfunctioning that evening.

Betty Stonorov's attorney led the questioning in the deposition of William Weston, the NTSB field investigator in charge of the captain's altimeter, a few months later. Shely was present but played a minor role. Weston testified that the altimeter was reading 225-250 feet too high at the time of the crash, that it was manufactured for the military, had no identifying marks, and had not been approved for use in civilian aviation. The FAA attorney raised the obvious question of sabotage and learned that it was the responsibility of the FBI to conduct an investigation, yet none was done.

Bluestone must have been aware of this, and it is unthinkable he wouldn't have told Woodcock and Fraser. Yet no public statement was made, no investigation was requested, and no record of this was located for over 50 years. The failure of Reuther's trusted associates and friends to seek justice for their murdered leader is inexplicable. In 2024, the leadership of the UAW was contacted with this new information concerning Reuther's death and did not respond. I also notified the Communications Department and the Media Inquiry page, and received no reply. The FBI and the NTSB doggedly persist in concealing the facts surrounding Reuther's death and the UAW remains silent.

The union Walter Reuther built was very much a product of a vicious battle in the late 30s and 40s for control of its future direction. I do not doubt that his maneuvering in those years was motivated by personal ambition. Still, principles were also involved, and who is to say that, as an individual, Reuther was any less principled than the other ambitious contenders for leadership? With his fertile mind, originality of thought, and reserves of energy to drive programs forward, Reuther was probably head and shoulders above his peers. Is there a single union president then or since who has had a more significant impact domestically?

Union leadership is something of a high-wire act. C. Wright Mills describes union leaders as "managers of discontent"—here whipping up expectations and generating militancy—there, with a deal in sight, going into reverse and entering a partnership with the employer to "sell" the agreed terms to the membership. It's an apt way of viewing what often happens in collective bargaining—an activity replete with grubby compromises. Reuther was an accomplished practitioner of the dark art of union leadership and achieved more than any other U.S. labor leader.[109] His assassination was a tragic loss for U.S. labor that has reverberated throughout the decades.

The assassination of Walter Reuther and his companions in 1970, and the lack of any thorough investigation for over five decades, raises serious questions about who has authority over history. Who gets to define or control historical narratives? Who tells history, and whose voices are privileged? Michel-Rolph Trouillot's *Silencing the Past: Power and the Production of History* is a pioneering work in historical theory and anthropology, first

109 I am grateful to Tony Carew for sharing his views on Reuther's achievements in collective bargaining and his role in the international field during the Cold War, with which I am broadly in agreement.

published in 1995. The book examines how power influences the creation, recording, and remembrance of history, focusing on the mechanisms by which certain events and voices are suppressed while others are amplified. Trouillot argues that history is not a neutral recounting of facts but is profoundly shaped by power dynamics at every stage of its production. He distinguishes between passive forgetting and active silencing. He contends that silencing is not merely the absence of information but often results from deliberate or structural processes that exclude some perspectives or events. These processes include erasure, trivialization, and the selective emphasis or omission of facts—and decisions about what is preserved influence what is remembered. Later interpretations frequently reinforce dominant power structures. History is about who controlled the past, and ultimately, who controls the future. Were those in power not only able to assassinate Reuther without turning him into a martyr, but were they also successful in diminishing his remarkable achievements?

Gifted historians have written volumes on Reuther, and those now sit comfortably on the shelf, establishing a paradigm on Reuther and U.S. labor. None of those tomes gave more than a fleeting rendering of his death. His assassination followed closely those of others he was politically connected to, John Kennedy, Martin Luther King Jr., and Robert Kennedy. Noble Prize-winning physicist Max Planck, a founder of quantum mechanics, described the phenomenon of paradigm in a way that applies to history: "A new scientific truth does not triumph by convincing its opponents and making them see the light, but rather because its opponents eventually die, and a new generation grows up that is familiar with it." The manner of Walter Reuther's death calls for a new examination and reassessment of him and his times.

Appendix I. Unite All Workers for Democracy

Reuther's bitter fights with Homer Martin and Jay Lovestone in the 1930s and the Communists from 1946 to 1949 led him to oppose all organized opposition in the UAW and adopt autocratic measures to accomplish this. The factional debate was effectively prohibited. His past experiences dominated his thinking, and he could not clearly see the future. The success of the small UAW reform group UAWD in transforming the UAW in 2022 demonstrates the importance of opposition groups and free, open debate in labor unions.

The Story of Unite All Workers for Democracy

By Scott Houldieson

Scott Houldieson, a 36-year member of UAW Local 551 in Chicago and a second-generation UAW member, started on the assembly line in the Trim Department at the Ford Chicago Assembly Plant. He became an UAW electrician apprentice in 1994. Houldieson was elected as an Alternate Committeeperson in 1998 and was appointed editor of the local union newspaper in 2006, serving on the newspaper committee until 2019. He was elected delegate to UAW Conventions in 2010, 2014, 2018, and 2022, and won elections as Financial Secretary in 2010 and Vice President in 2015. He was a founding member of Unite All Workers for Democracy, and he chaired the caucus from 2020 to 2025.

July 26, 2017, the U.S. Department of Justice released a grand jury indictment charging Iacobelli, the former Vice President for Employee Relations for Fiat Chrysler, and Monica Morgan, the widow of former UAW International Vice President General Holiefield, with conspiracy to extract 1.2 million dollars from the UAW-Chrysler National Training Center and divert it to General Holiefield and his girlfriend/wife Monica Morgan. Money was laundered through the Leave the Light On Foundation charity controlled by Holiefield and paid to businesses owned by Monica Morgan. The Leave the Light On Foundation was supposed to "help children struggling with hardships." Instead, most of the funds donated by the UAW-Chrysler National Training Center to the foundation were paid to businesses owned by Monica Morgan.

According to U.S. Department of Justice officials, the money diverted to Holiefield and other UAW officials were bribes designed to keep the union officials "fat, dumb, and happy" in the 2011 and 2015 contract talks. The bribes were also designed to improve the company's enforcement of the contract between negotiations. This all clouded contract negotiations between 2009 and 2015. High-ranking union officials sold out autoworkers.

By the end of January 2018, Alphons Iacobelli, along with Fiat Chrysler financial analyst Jerome Durden and UAW Administrative Assistant Virdell King, had pled guilty to his part in the conspiracy. In June of that year, the UAW would gather in Detroit for its quadrennial Constitutional Convention.

The 2018 UAW Constitutional Convention would prove interesting. UAW International Vice President Norwood Jewell, who was responsible for the beleaguered Chrysler Department, abruptly resigned and retired at the end of 2017. Region 9 Director Terry Dittes was appointed to fill the remainder of the term.

This convention was held under the cloud of the unfolding corruption scandal. Norwood Jewell was noticeably absent from the convention. In many ways, it was no different from past conventions. The normalcy of it all while sitting under this cloud of corruption was unsettling. When I attempted to amend the Convention Rules to allow for greater democracy and had many seconds to my proposed amendment, President Dennis Williams said: "Okay, first we are going to do the first motion. Right. We have a motion on the floor of the rules. And if we do not pass that motion, then we will come back and entertain your motion." I said: "No, the amendment should be in order on the motion."

President Williams told me: "Scott, for one thing, these rules have been in place forever. So, let's go to Robert's Rules of Order. First of all, the motion was made by the committee. It was supported by the body. That motion has to go into effect. And then, if that motion does not clear, we will come back and entertain it. Otherwise, you are out of order."

I responded: "Well, I would recommend that the rules be voted down so that we can address this problem, because it has been a problem at previous conventions. If you recall, at the bargaining convention, I made a similar motion to amend a report. That motion to amend the report by one word, from "bridge the gap" to "eliminate the gap" was denied because of this rule. That's undemocratic, and it needs to change. So, I recommend that the delegation vote these rules down so that we can make this correction to the rules and enhance the democratic processes of our union."

President Williams said: "Well, brother, I happen to disagree. We will find out if the body disagrees. Okay, all right, and then when I retire, I am going to sit down and you and I need to have a long talk."

Despite the publicly exposed bribery scheme, Williams and the Administration Caucus expected to run this convention no differently than past conventions. Elected delegates, for the most part, were on board with the status quo. No reforms were forthcoming at the 2018 UAW Convention. Although more contested than in previous conventions, the transfer of power went off without a hitch. Dennis Williams retired and handed the reins over to Gary Jones. Jones's ascent to the top position in the UAW took a different route than usual. All previous UAW International Presidents had held national office before being tapped for the top job. Jones was different. He went from being the Director of UAW Region 5 to President. It took a little over a year before the world learned how this maneuver was accomplished.

The Founding of UAWD

On August 28, 2019, news broke that federal agents launched coordinated raids in six locations across four states aimed at top UAW officials, including the homes of the sitting International President, Gary Jones, and his immediate predecessor, President Dennis Williams. This occurred in the middle of the Big contract negotiations.

On September 12, 2019, charges were filed in Federal Court against the sitting Regional Director of UAW Region 5, Vance Pearson. The charging document concealed the names of four co-conspirators, naming them UAW Official A, B, C & D. It became clear after reading the account in the charging document that UAW Official A was Gary Jones, and UAW Official B was Dennis Williams. It was less clear who UAW Official C & D were.

By this time, activist UAW members had been discussing the corruption scandal for a couple of years. The revelation of the raids on the homes of Gary Jones and Dennis Williams, along with raids at the Black Lake UAW Education Center, UAW Region 5 headquarters in Hazelwood, Missouri, the home of UAW Region 5 Director Vance Pearson, and the Wisconsin home of one of Dennis Williams top assistants during his time in office refocused the UAW membership away from contract negotiations and back on the expanding corruption scandal.

On September 18, 2019, I received a Facebook Messenger direct message from Brian Schneck, the President of UAW Local 259 in New York. The message simply said "Article 30 Section 1b)." I responded with the message and "Article 8 Section 4(2)." Brian's point was that the membership needed to file charges against the sitting President of the UAW. Article 30 of the UAW Constitution is titled Charges and Trials of International Officers. Brian was finding a local union to get the charges started.

International Officers can be put on trial for misconduct in two ways.

1. With an affidavit signed by at least 5 UAW International Executive Board members submitted to the Secretary-Treasurer.

2. With a signed affidavit by a member in good standing and endorsed by a majority vote of those members at a local union meeting and endorsed by a majority vote of at least 10 other local unions. (The UAW Constitution has since been amended to reduce the number of endorsing local unions to 5.)

I informed Brian that I had been lobbying locals nationwide to pass a resolution to call a Special Convention to change how we elect our International Officers. I responded to Brian's inquiry with the Article 8 Section 4(2) reference. The hurdles to calling a Special Convention in this way are high. Calling a Special Convention by the membership is done through a referendum process. First, it requires passing a resolution demanding a Special Convention stating the reason or reasons why such a Convention is desired, the place and date for the Convention and the dates for mailing out and returning the referendum ballots. At least fifteen local unions must pass this resolution in five different states representing not less than twenty percent of the total membership as reported at the preceding Constitutional Convention. This is a very heavy organizing lift. We were determined to make it happen.

I invited Brian to participate in a conference call that Friday. He asked if his Vice President, Michael DiGiuseppe, could participate instead because he had a prior engagement.

At the conference call on Friday, September 20, 2019, Chris Budnick, Michael DiGiuseppe, Chris Laursen, Ken Larew, Travis Watkins, Justin Mayhugh, Joe Valentine, and Jessie Kelly. We discussed how to hold UAW officials accountable. We talked about the UAW Constitution Article 30 – Trials of International Officers. We also noted that many of those involved were not or no longer were International Officers. For those, we needed to find another article.

Article 32 – Public Review Board covers complaints about violations of UAW Ethical Practices Codes. This would allow us to demand that the UAW International Executive Board put those out of reach of most rank-and-file members on trial. The International Executive Board has the ability under Article 31 Section 20 to file those charges but chose not to. We also discussed the process for calling a Special Convention through membership action. The Article 8 Section 4(2) process would be a heavy lift. Still, we hoped to get the membership to make much-needed reforms in our union before the Federal Government decided to take over the UAW.

Chris Budnick, a tier-two worker at the huge Ford Kentucky Truck Plant, took the lead on the Article 30 charges. In October 2019, in consultation with his UAW Local 862 President, Todd Dunn, he created an affidavit charging the sitting President of the UAW, Gary Jones, and the sitting Director of Region 5, Vance Pearson, with conduct unbecoming a union member. The charges included what was laid out in the September 12th Federal charges against Vance Pearson.

For charges and a trial to commence, Chris' affidavit had to be approved by his local union at their monthly membership meetings, which took place in two sessions—one for each shift. Chris' affidavit would need to be endorsed by at least ten other local unions at their membership meetings.[110] Chris presented the affidavit at his October 2019 union meeting. It passed at the first and failed to pass at the second. Chris tried again at the November 12, 2019 Local 862 membership meetings. This time both meetings approved it.

Just over a week later, on November 20th, the *Detroit News* covered the effort by UAW members to charge Jones and Pearson in a front-page article.[111] Five additional local unions had already endorsed the charges against Jones and Pearson. In

110 The UAW Constitution was subsequently amended to decrease the number of endorsing local unions from 10 to 5 at the 2022 Constitutional Convention as one of the conditions of the Consent Decree.

111 https://www.detroitnews.com/story/business/autos/2019/11/19/uaw-locals-remove-president-gary-jones/4232490002/?fbclid=IwAR1kyDqCyH6dwtw-T0_xFPYUkhWlGu2OYY4lJJuQnZCnOK-67d2DOXXZf0M

addition to Local 862, Locals 774, 259, 1596, 7770, and 7902 had endorsed the charges. Brian Schneck, the President of Local 259, had lobbied other locals in Region 9A to endorse the charges. By the end of the day, the UAW International Executive Board finally found the courage to file their own charges against Gary Jones and Vance Pearson.

Another accountability measure would be changing the way we elect our International Officers. Since its founding, the UAW has elected our International Officers by electing delegates to the UAW Constitutional Convention who vote on behalf of their members. Between 1947 and 2022, the same caucus has controlled nearly all seats on the UAW International Executive Board. In 1947 Walter Reuther's caucus swept the International Executive Board elections, then consolidated those wins to concentrate their power. They used the anti-communist sentiment in the country to expel potential opposition to the caucus. That concentration of power and lack of accountability in our union led to deeply embedded corruption.

Our effort to call a Special Convention to change how we elect our International Officer to a One Member One Vote system was gaining traction in late 2019 and early 2020. We were concerned that we needed to move as fast as we could with this organizing. We felt the Federal Government was on the verge of taking over our union. The Vance Pearson charging papers clearly laid out the case for conspiracy and a Racketeering Influenced and Corrupt Organization (RICO) suit. We wanted to take control of our union before the Federal Government did. The initial resolution set the date for mailing referendum ballots for February 21, 2020. We were running out of time to reach the 20% threshold, so in February of 2020, we did a reset and extended the deadline to February 21, 2021.

As mentioned before, there was a high threshold for triggering a referendum to call that convention. By March of 2020, we had surpassed the number of Locals needed. We had 24 Local Unions who had passed a version of the Special Convention resolution, surpassing the 15 Local Unions required in Article 8 Section 4(2). These Local Unions were located in Michigan, New York, Iowa, Ohio, Kentucky, Tennessee, Massachusetts, and Missouri, surpassing the five states required in the Constitution. Where we were still lacking was the twenty percent threshold. These 24 local unions represented around 58,400 members. The total UAW membership, as reported in the 2017 LM2 report was 395,703. The 20 percent threshold would have been 79,141.

We were well on our way when, in March 2020, the COVID-19 global pandemic led to lockdowns. For more than a year, in-person gatherings were canceled. Our organizing for a Special Convention hit an insurmountable roadblock.

We continued to work towards holding corrupt officials accountable. Many offenders were out of the reach of charges under Article 30 since this is only for sitting International Officers. For the most part, Article 31 charges are available to hold members of one's own local union accountable. The International Executive Board has the authority to bring charges under Article 31 Section 20: "In cases of extreme emergency and when it appears to the International Executive Board that irreparable injury may result to the International Union or to a subordinate body from offenses punishable under this Constitution... the Board may, if two-thirds (2/3) of its members concur, prefer charges against such member or members for the violation of this Constitution or for conduct unbecoming a member of the Union."

The UAW International Executive Board could have used Article 31 Section 20 at any time since the federal charges started dropping, and they could also have used it at any time those charged started pleading guilty. But they didn't.

In a letter dated October 28, 2019, I filed an Article 32 complaint stating that IEB members had violated the UAW Ethical Practices Codes. The letter stated the following:

> President Jones,
>
> I, Scott Houldieson, a member in good standing with Local 551 hereby file this complaint related to the Ethical Practices Code – Financial Practices – in accordance with Article 32 Section 5 b with the Public Review Board.
>
> International President of the UAW, Gary Jones, in collusion with Vance Pearson Region 5 Director

and former President Dennis Williams, violated the Ethical Practices Code of the UAW Constitution by engaging in the embezzlement of union funds, filing false LM reports and maintaining false union records, mail and wire fraud, money laundering, aiding and abetting, conspiracy all of which are serious violations of the Labor-Management Reporting and Disclosure Act, (LMRDA). These violations were exposed in the attached criminal complaint filed against Region 5 Director Vance Pearson by Special Agent Andrew Donahue, U.S. Department of Labor on or about September 12, 2019.

This reckless, outrageous and self-serving conduct has not only brought a swirl of controversy, shame and embarrassment to our UAW but also the known and unknown monetary costs which threatens the financial position of the Union as it's certain that financial resources will be necessarily spent from the union's treasury in order to protect and preserve the integrity of the UAW. These monetary resources were originally purposed for organizing, collective bargaining and to provide services to each member of the UAW thus, this in its itself is a theft from the membership.

In addition to the above allegations there have been multiple guilty pleas entered in the widening corruption probe being conducted by the Department of Labor and the Internal Revenue Service. Jeff Pietrzyk and Mike Grimes have plead guilty to bribery and kickbacks that also implicate former Vice President Joe Ashton. Former Vice President Norwood Jewell has plead guilty to taking bribes from representatives of FCA and to misappropriation of union funds. Also pleading guilty in the FCA portion of the investigation are Nancy Adams Johnson, Keith Mickens, Virdell King, and the wife of deceased Vice President General Holiefield.

Failure of the UAW International Executive Board to deal with these blatant violations of the UAW Constitution leaves it up to the UAW membership to use our authority under the UAW Constitution to seek justice.

This is filed without the approval of my local union because we lacked a quorum to conduct official business on both the September 21, 2019, and October 19, 2019, general membership meetings. Further delay would exceed the time limits established in Article 32 Section 4.

I'm requesting appropriate redress. Considering the seriousness of the charges nothing short of a recommendation of revocation of membership in the UAW to all of the officers, former officers, and officials involved with these violations of the Ethical Practices Codes are appropriate remedies.

It's the expectation that President Jones shall facilitate and carry out his obligations under Section 32 Section 5(b) and forward a copy to the International Executive Board and a copy to the Chairperson of the Public Review Board without delay.

In Solidarity,
Scott Houldieson

cc: Executive Director Public Review Board, Carmen Parcelli, Public Review Board members; Dean Harry C. Katz, Professor Maria L. Ontiveros, Professor Janice R. Bellace, Professor James J. Brudney, Region 4 Director Ron McInroy

I received a response from the UAW International Executive Board on June 1, 2020. They indicated that after receiving my Article 32 Complaint (January 31, 2019) it took another 93 days to file charges against former Vice Presidents Ashton and Jewell and former staffers Grimes, Johnson, King, Mickens and Robinson. They still refused to file charges against former President Williams. They said, "Former UAW President Williams has not been charged with any wrongdoing..."

I appealed their decision not to charge Dennis Williams to the UAW Public Review Board.

During the fall of 2019, we also considered creating an organization that could last beyond the latest corruption scandal. In late October 2019, we were tossing around different ideas about what to call this organization. Under consideration were: Workers for a Democratic Union, Autoworkers for a Democratic Union, UAW for a Democratic Union, Members for a Democratic Union, United Autoworkers for Democratic Justice, Workers for Self Determination, Solidarity Network, and Unite All Workers for Democracy. We polled the 30 or so workers involved with our organizing against corruption. Unite All Workers for Democracy (UAWD) was chosen for our name.

We started working on governing documents for UAWD. Teamsters for a Democratic Union (TDU) was a caucus within the International Brotherhood of Teamsters. TDU has a constitution as its governing document. They had won the right to vote in a 1989 consent decree that resulted from a RICO suit aimed at removing organized crime influence from their union. TDU lobbied the federal government for this reform as part of their consent decree.

We also looked at a reform movement in the UAW from the same era. New Directions was a UAW caucus that challenged the Reuther Caucus in the mid to late 1980s. UAW legend Jerry Tucker ran for UAW Region 5 Director at the 1986 UAW Constitutional Convention. His election was stolen. By this time, the Reuther Caucus was also known as the Administration Caucus. They recruited some union officers to attend as delegates whose locals had not held delegate elections. Tucker appealed the election to the US Department of Labor. The election was overturned and in a special convention, he was elected Region 5 Director for the remainder of the term. We got our hands on a copy of the New Directions Constitution.

With these two documents, in November of 2019 we started drafting a Constitution for UAWD. There were members of our group who didn't see the value in having governing documents. They were only working with us to further their goal of electing Brian Keller as UAW International President. They went from attacking the UAW International to attacking those of us working to build a long-lasting reform movement in the UAW. We knew that changing the UAW would never be accomplished as a single event. It is a generational endeavor, and we needed an organization that would last for decades, just as TDU had done.

Travis Watkins, Chris Budnick, Ken Larew and I worked together to assemble a draft Constitution. By early December 2019, we had put together a framework. We began planning a UAW National Convention/Meeting where we could approve the document and elect officers. Our target was the Labor Notes Conference scheduled for April 17-19, 2020, in Chicago, although there was also some support for holding it in the fall of 2020. Eventually, we landed on having bylaws rather than a Constitution to deflect any charge of dual unionism.

Feds file Anti-Corruption, Anti-Fraud suit

On December 14, 2020, the Federal Government filed suit against the UAW under a federal law aimed at fighting corruption and fraud. That same day, U.S. Attorney Matthew Schneider and UAW International President Rory Gamble held a joint press conference to announce that the suit was settled under the terms of a Consent Decree agreed to by the UAW and the U.S. Department of Justice.

The Consent Decree had several provisions. Included among those provisions was the appointment of a Federal Monitor to oversee the union for six years and a referendum vote of the entire UAW membership to decide how the UAW International Executive Board (IEB) would be elected in the future. Would we continue to elect the IEB by electing delegates to vote on our behalf (the Delegate Election System)? Or would we change to offering every member of the UAW the right to cast a vote (the Direct Voting System)?

UAWD filed a motion to intervene in the case, but our motion was denied. We had hoped to have the right to directly elect simply written into the Consent Decree. Instead, we would have to organize a referendum. We were very disappointed that we would have to jump through this hoop. As it turns out, the referendum was a blessing in disguise. It forced us to organize our fellow UAW members.

Our motion to intervene was denied; however, by filing it, we had the opportunity to consult with the Monitor and the Elections Staff to ensure a free and fair election process.

Some of us had done local in plant organizing in one form or another. Some of us had mounted vote no campaigns against bad contracts. Some of us had organized to run for local union offices. A few of us had organized to run candidates for International Executive Board under the delegate election system. The referendum vote would be a national campaign unlike any we had done before. We needed help.

On April 12, 2021, Lisa Xu began working as a contract staff organizer for UAWD. Lisa had been an organizer for Local 5118 until earlier that year. We didn't know how we would afford to pay Lisa but we took a leap of faith. As it turned out, our staff have been adept at fundraising.

We launched our campaign to win the referendum with a "Week of Action" to coincide with the Battle of the Overpass anniversary at the Ford Rouge Complex. May 19th we passed out flyers at Local 2250 near the GM Wentzville Assembly Plant. We held a phone bank to get flyers to union activists nationwide. We passed out flyers at the GM Lansing Delta Township plant until the police were called on us. We passed more out at the Ford Dearborn Truck Plant. The next week we passed them out at Ford Chicago Assembly Plant and Ford Chicago Stamping Plant. I was getting thousands of flyers printed at a union print shop near my house and sending them around the country.

While we were passing out flyers, we also shared information about how to attend the sentencing hearings for former UAW Presidents Dennis Williams (May 11, 2021) and Gary Jones (June 10, 2021). These were virtual hearings, and we shared the registration links widely.

We spent all summer campaigning for One Member One Vote. Then the Monitor's election team settled on the phrase "Direct Voting System or Delegate Voting System" for the ballot choices. Ballots for the referendum would be mailed out on October 19, 2021. They were due back by November 29, 2021.

We couldn't afford to send postcards to every UAW member, and there were around a million potential voters. So, we mailed colorful postcards to a percentage of members in some locals with whom we had not made contact. In all, we sent around 70,000 postcards.

The UAW had vastly more resources than our start up caucus could gather. The postcards they sent out were in small blue print that was hard to read. They sent postcards out advertising the referendum only once, on August 27, 2021. This was more about testing the validity of the mailing list as it was an advertisement for the referendum.

Approximately 1.3 million ballots were printed.[112] There were 140,586 ballots returned that were deemed eligible voters. The ballots were counted on December 2, 2021, at a facility in Hamden Connecticut. UAWD had observers there for the count, including Bill Parker, Mike Cannon, Lisa Xu and Nathan Pensler. The Direct Voting System garnered 89,615 votes (63.7%) while the Delegate Voting System garnered 50,971 votes (36.3%). The UAW was now poised to have Direct Elections for our International Executive Board members for the first time in our history! A dream of generations of UAW activists was about to become a reality.

The Search for Candidates and Election Rules

The referendum victory was just a step in a long road towards reform in the UAW. Democratic elections without candidates is no democracy at all. In 1996 the Laborers International Union of North America (LIUNA) held their first direct election for the top two union officers.[113] This also included a referendum of members to decide if they preferred to directly elect the remaining General Executive Board officers. The referendum switched the union to the direct election system. The first direct elections for the top two union officers, the General President and General Secretary-Treasurer, resulted in the "Old Guard" remaining in office. Incumbent President Arthur Coia won with 67% of the vote

112 According to the Monitor's referendum report. 2021 UAW Referendum Final Rules (11.8.2021) - 8pm

113 LIUNA entered in to a Consent Decree to settle a RICO suit in February 1995. Several reforms were required including direct election for the top two union officers and a referendum to allow LIUNA members to decide if the rest of the General Executive Board would be directly elected as well. Laborers-LIUNA Election Officer Report-1966 LIUNA Election

and the General Secretary Treasurer, R. P. Vinall was reelected by acclamation when no candidates ran against him. The "Old Guard" maintained control throughout the ensuing 15 years of direct elections. Terry O'Sullivan was appointed General President upon Coia's retirement and retained that position until his retirement in 2023. The delegates at the 2011 Convention voted to return to the Convention's system of electing LIUNA General Executive Board officers.

The UAWD Steering Committee knew we had to find viable candidates to run for the UAW International Executive Board, or we would eventually lose the One Member, One Vote victory. We created a process for candidate recruitment and endorsement and established a subcommittee for the IEB Candidate Search.

Ensuring a Fair First Election

We also knew that having fair election rules would be critical to the success of the newly won One Member One Vote election process. While we were searching for candidates we also engaged with the Monitor's election team to make sure the election rules would level the playing field. Incumbents always have an advantage in elections. We didn't want that advantage to be insurmountable for viable challengers.

We recommended keeping a low bar for ballot access. The Convention system only required one delegate at the Constitutional Convention to place someone into nomination. We suggested keeping ballot access relatively easy. They took our suggestion and kept the single delegate nomination requirement to get on the ballot.

We recommended slate voting. While the UAW Constitution has some barriers to slate names in Local Union elections the Administration Caucus, at the 2018 Constitutional Convention adopted a rule allowing slate voting at that convention. The Monitor's election team took our suggestion and allowed slate names to appear on the ballot.

We recommended public funding of campaigns to level the playing field. We argued that the Administration Caucus would have a large contingent of highly paid staff to rely on for funding their campaign. Our recommendation for public funding was rejected. The Monitor landed on a true source and true source and true purpose rules. These rules required campaigns to create a paper trail through disclosure forms that report donors, the amount of the donations and contact info so the Monitor could verify the donation was explicitly for the UAW International Officer elections. Donation guidelines were those the Labor Management Reporting and Disclosure Act (LMRDA) requires in union elections.

We recommended requiring majority vote to win election tilizing Ranked Choice Voting (RCV) with an instant runoff system. This would allow voters to rank their favored candidates while saving time and expense of resending runoff ballots for a second election round. The Monitor decided to put this question to the delegates at the 2022 UAW Constitutional Convention. UAWD aligned delegates argued in favor of RCV but the Administration Caucus was squarely opposed to this method. The delegates voted to reject RCV at the 2022 Convention.

Steering Our Caucus

We started out as something like a network when we began our work to reform the UAW. We met via conference calls. At a conference call on January 12, 2020 we voted to have Travis Watkins from Local 167 in Wyoming, Michigan as the Financial Secretary and Joseph Valentine from Local 31 in Fairfax, Kansas as the Primary Officer. Other members in attendance were Scott Houldieson from Local 551 in Chicago, Illinois, Justin Mayhugh from Local 31 in Fairfax, Kansas, Teri Norris from Local 1250 in Cleveland, Ohio, Chris Budnick from Local 862 in Louisville, Kentucky, Kenneth Larew from Local 1853 in Spring Hill, Tennessee. We made plans to open a bank account for UAWD.

Panning for Gold

We created a process for endorsing candidates for the upcoming UAW International Executive Board elections. A committee of mostly UAWD Steering Committee members, dubbed the IEB Endorsement Preparations Committee, would do outreach and vetting of potential candidates in the first ever

Direct Elections in the UAW. Members of UAWD could also submit names of potential candidates to the Steering Committee for consideration by the Endorsement Preparations Committee. The Committee was tasked with finding potential candidates. They would then make recommendations on potential candidates to the UAWD Steering Committee. Candidates would proceed to a formal endorsement process in one of two ways: 1. A majority vote of the Steering Committee 2. Two or more UAWD members recommend a candidate to the Steering Committee.

Once in the formal endorsement process, candidates would fill out a detailed candidate questionnaire. The questionnaire and answers would be shared with all UAWD members. Candidates may also meet with the Steering Committee, and if they do, the notes or recording of the meeting will be shared with the UAWD membership. Candidates would then be asked to meet with the UAWD membership, where they could ask follow-up questions. After this meeting, there would be a UAWD membership meeting to which the candidates would not be invited, and members could debate whether or not to endorse the candidates for the positions they were seeking.

There were three rounds of endorsements. The first candidates who went through this process were Margaret Mock seeking an endorsement for UAW International Secretary Treasurer, LaShawn English seeking an endorsement for UAW Region 1 Director. They were formally endorsed by UAWD on June 12, 2022. The second round of endorsements was for the office of UAW International President. On July 17, 2022 UAWD endorsed Shawn Fain for UAW International President. The third and final round of endorsements took place after the UAW Constitutional Convention. On August 7, 2022 four candidates were under consideration for endorsement. Mike Booth for UAW International Vice President, Rich Boyer for UAW International Vice President, Daniel Vicente for UAW Region 9 Director and Brandon Mancilla for UAW Region 9A Director.

All seven of these candidates were endorsed and the campaign got underway. We were proud to have pulled together a diverse slate of qualified UAW members. All had served in bargaining or administration of their local unions at one time or another. Shawn Fain had also been on UAW International Staff. He was now in a position of running against his boss, incumbent UAW International President Ray Curry. LaShawn, and Rich had both been on Chrysler or FCA National Negotiating teams. Mike, Brandon and Daniel had been involved with local contract negotiations and Brandon was one of the founding members of his Local Union – UAW Local 5118 – The Harvard Graduate Workers Union. Margaret had been a Financial Secretary at UAW Local 961.

Their first decision as a slate was what the slate name would be. Naturally the Unite All Workers for Democracy slate was a proposal, but to appeal to UAW members who might not have known about UAWD or had a negative impression of UAWD the slate decided on a more inclusive name. They decided on UAW Members United.

UAWD members launched wholeheartedly into the UAW Members United campaign. We hosted phone banks and fundraisers. Our first fundraiser was at the Anchor Bar in Detroit during the 38th UAW Constitutional Convention. We printed several hundred thousand flyers for distribution at UAW shops around the country. Shawn, Margaret, Mike and Rich toured the Midwest and South meeting members at campaign events UAWD members and our Staff helped set up.

At locals where we did not have union activists to distribute campaign literature we sent postcards to a percentage of members utilizing the election vendor's global mailing list. We also utilized the UAW mass email service set up for the election. UAWD Staff, Lisa Xu and Nathan Pensler, were on loan to the campaign and helped produce the UAW Members United ads for the UAW's official publication – *Solidarity Magazine*. Nathan was the campaign manager and Lisa provided support with just about every aspect of the campaign from Social Media to Graphic Design for flyers, postcards, emails, etc.

The UAW Monitor hosted Candidate Forums for Presidential, Secretary, Treasurer, and Vice Presidential candidates. Our Steering Committee and Staff helped prep the UAW Members United candidates for the forums. Labor writer Steven Greenhouse was the moderator for all three candidate forums. The UAW Members United candidates all did extremely well with the forums.

As the campaigns were coming to a close in mid November 2022 the Steering Committee and Staff were wondering how this first election would turn out. Some of us thought we would be lucky to get one or two wins. We had even asked potential candidates how they would function as a minority on the International Executive Board. I was a little more optimistic. I felt this would be a change election and that we could pick up four or five spots on the IEB. None of us envisioned what would happen at the count in Dayton, Ohio.

The tally of votes began the Tuesday after Thanksgiving, November 29, 2022 and continued through Friday December 2, 2022.

Observers were allowed to watch every aspect of the count. Some ballots had to be looked at because a voter changed their mind and marked out their original choice and colored in their final choice. The election contractor along with the Monitor's election staff would make a determination. Observers were able to challenge that determination if they had an argument that the determination was made in error. Of the thousands of ballots that were processed a miniscule amount needed to be scrutinized this way.

The count began following the Thanksgiving weekend. UAWD had a running tally we kept up on our website as votes were counted. The process was that ballots from locals were separated into separate mail bins. Small locals would have a single bin, sometimes with a handful of ballots in it. Larger locals might have a dozen or more mail bins with ballots in them. The ballots from a local would stay together through the whole process. Envelopes where the membership status of the voter could not be verified immediately or envelopes with similar names were flagged for further investigation.

First the outer envelopes would be opened with a slitting machine. These envelopes have voter identifying information on them. To provide voter secrecy the voter was supposed to put their completed ballot into a secrecy envelope that was provided before mailing it back. After they were opened they would be put back into mail bins and transferred to a table where workers would remove the secrecy envelope from the mailing envelope.

Mailing envelopes would go into one bin and secrecy envelopes with the ballots would go into another bin.

Workers would then inspect the ballots looking for damaged ballots or ballots with stray marks on them. They were looking for anything that might be a problem for the machines to count the ballots. Ballots that were damaged in any way would go to a table to be fixed. This process was called curing. Observers from every candidate or slate were able to watch the process of ballots being cured to make sure the election workers were marking the duplicate ballot exactly as the voter had intended.

The Regional Director winners were announced as the results were tabulated. Five Regions were won by acclamation. Those were Laura Dickerson Region 1A, Steve Dawes Region 1D, Brandon Campbell Region 4, Mike Miller Region 6, and Tim Smith Region 8.

There were contested elections in four regions. In Region 1; LaShawn English for the UAW Members United slate and James Harris for the Curry Solidarity Team were on the ballot. LaShawn won 7,785 to 7,011. In Region 2B; Dave Green, an independent candidate and Wayne Blanchard for the Curry Solidarity Team were on the ballot. Dave won 12,064 to 8,363. In Region 9A Brandon Mancilla for the UAW Members United slate and Beverly Brakeman for the Curry Solidarity Team were on the ballot. Brandon won 2,562 to 1,852. In Region 9 there were three candidates vying for the Director position. Jimmy Lakeman ran as an independent candidate, Lauren Farrell for the Curry Solidarity Team and Daniel Vicente for the UAW Members United slate were on the ballot. That race went to a runoff between Daniel Vicente who had the highest vote total.

The Secretary Treasurer race was a landslide. Margaret Mock for the UAW Members United slate and Frank Stuglin for the Curry Solidarity Team were the two candidates. Margaret won every region. The final tally was 63,121 for Margaret Mock and 38,813 for Frank Stuglin.

The Vice President's race featured eight candidates running for three positions. Independent candidates were: Sharon Bell, Rich LeTourneau and Mike Turner. UAW Members United had two candidates: Mike Booth and Rich Boyer. The Curry Solidarity Team had three candidates: Tim Bressler, Chuck

Browning and Bryan Czape. To achieve a majority in a race with three positions you take the total votes cast, divide by the number of positions then divide by two. That gives you the 50% threshold. Add one more vote and that is the number required to win on the first ballot. Mike Booth received the most votes, 44,902. Mike was announced as elected fairly late in the count. Rich Boyer came in second with 43,629 votes. At the end of the last day for the count Rich was close to having enough to be declared winner without a runoff. After curing some challenged ballots Rich picked up enough votes to be declared elected. That left Chuck Browning with 39,435 votes and Tim Bressler with 35,632 votes in a runoff for the third Vice President position. The remaining vote totals were: Bryan Czape, 29,454 votes; Sharon Bell, 28,276 votes; Mike Turner, 22,835 votes; and Rich LeTourneau 16, 025 votes.

The race for UAW International President featured five candidates. Independent candidates were Brian Keller, Mark Gibson and Will Lehman who was backed by the World Socialist Website folks. Shawn Fain was the candidate leading the UAW Members United slate and Ray Curry was the incumbent President. He led the Curry Solidarity Team. No candidate won a majority of the votes. Ray Curry had the lead with 39,572 votes. He would face Shawn Fain in a runoff. Shawn had 38,958 votes in the first round. The remaining vote totals were 14,561 for Brian Keller, 5,627 for Mark Gibson and 4,777 for Will Lehman.

As we approached the holiday season of 2022-2023, we started making plans for the runoff elections. Two candidates from the UAW Members United slate were on the runoff ballot, and we felt hopeful going into the runoff. In the Region 9 Director race, Daniel held a 616-vote lead over Lauren Farrell, the candidate from the Curry Solidarity Team. Although Jimmy Lakeman had withdrawn from the race, he received 1,846 votes in the first round. Lakeman's votes were up for grabs, and he endorsed Farrell in the runoff.

Shawn Fain was a close second to the incumbent Ray Curry in the race for International President. Only 614 votes separated the two candidates, and nearly 25,000 votes went to the other three candidates. Shawn did a Facebook live with Brian Keller, and Keller gave Shawn an endorsement.

On December 12, 2022 the prevailing candidates were sworn into office. Those included Secretary-Treasurer Margaret Mock, Vice President Mike Booth, Vice President Rich Boyer, Region 1 Director LaShawn English, Region 1A Director Laura Dickerson who was unopposed in the election, Region 1D Director Steve Dawes who was also unopposed, Region 2B Director Dave Green, Region 4 Director Brandon Campbell who had been unopposed, Region 6 Director Mike Miller who was unopposed, Region 8 Director Tim Smith who was unopposed and Region 9A Director Brandon Mancilla.

In the weeks following the initial round of the election, we planned fundraisers, produced endorsement videos, and designed flyers for printing. After the New Year, we entered full campaign mode again. We had flyers printed and distributed them to union activists at as many locals as possible. Chris Budnick and I accompanied Shawn Fain and Nathan Pensler on a southern campaign swing visiting plants in Kentucky, Tennessee, and Ohio. We also sent out a number of postcards to a portion of the workers at UAW Locals where we were experiencing difficulties reaching voters.

One big difference with the runoff was the fact that the UAW International was suddenly very interested in making voters aware of the runoff election. They sent five postcard reminders to vote between December 2, 2022 and the end of February 2023. The races still to be decided were International President, one International Vice President and Region 9 Director.

The tally took place in Dayton, Ohio once again. The tally started March 1, 2023. By mid-day on March 1, the race for Region 9 Director was announced for Daniel Vicente. Daniel had 4,349 votes while Lauren Farrell received 4,030 votes. The Vice President race featured two candidates from the same slate. Chuck Browning and Tim Bressler, both from the Curry Solidarity Team faced one another in the runoff. However, Bressler had stopped campaigning and was supporting Browning. Voters were not necessarily aware of this fact. As votes came in Bressler was receiving votes but Browning was clearly headed towards victory. The margin became big enough early on March 4th. Browning was the presumed winner.

Vote counting continued and by the end of the day on Saturday March 4, 2023 the UAW International President race was too close to call. Shawn Fain was in the lead with 69,118 votes to Ray Curry's 68,473 votes. With around 1,600 ballots where the voter eligibility was in question, Shawn led by 645 votes.

The remaining 1,600 ballots were taken to a secure location in Taylor, Michigan where several rounds of voter verifications were conducted. On March 25, 2023 Shawn Fain was declared the winner by a razor thin margin of 483 votes. Shawn Fain was sworn in as the first UAW International President elected by direct vote of the UAW membership on Sunday, March 26, 2023. His first task would be to chair the UAW Special Bargaining Convention, which would commence the following day. It was a Convention planned by former President Curry and attended by 661 delegates from across the UAW, many of whom supported his opponent in the just concluded election.

Appendix II. FBI Documents

The memo below was addressed to D. J. Brennan, with a copy and enclosure sent to C. D. Brennan.

D. J. Brennan Jr. was an FBI agent who served in the Bureau during the 1960s. While there, he was involved with the Internal Security Section, which, among other things, dealt with matters concerning U.S. nationals in Cuba.

C. D. Brennan served as the Chief of the Internal Security Section within the FBI, as indicated by his participation in high-level communications and meetings. He was involved in counterintelligence and domestic surveillance operations, and his responsibilities included interagency coordination. He attended meetings with the CIA Director and other intelligence officials.

Some of the names of those who received copies of this document are redacted, and next to one of those names is written "61." Exemption 6 of the Freedom of Information Act pertains to privacy, while "exemption 1" relates to national security.

Images used in this section courtesy of the WJBK-TV collection, the Walter P. Reuther Library, Wayne State University. There are 59 documents in this 1967–1970 file. WJBK-TV was the TV station Bill Gallagher worked for.

Walter Reuther. Security Matter — Communist.

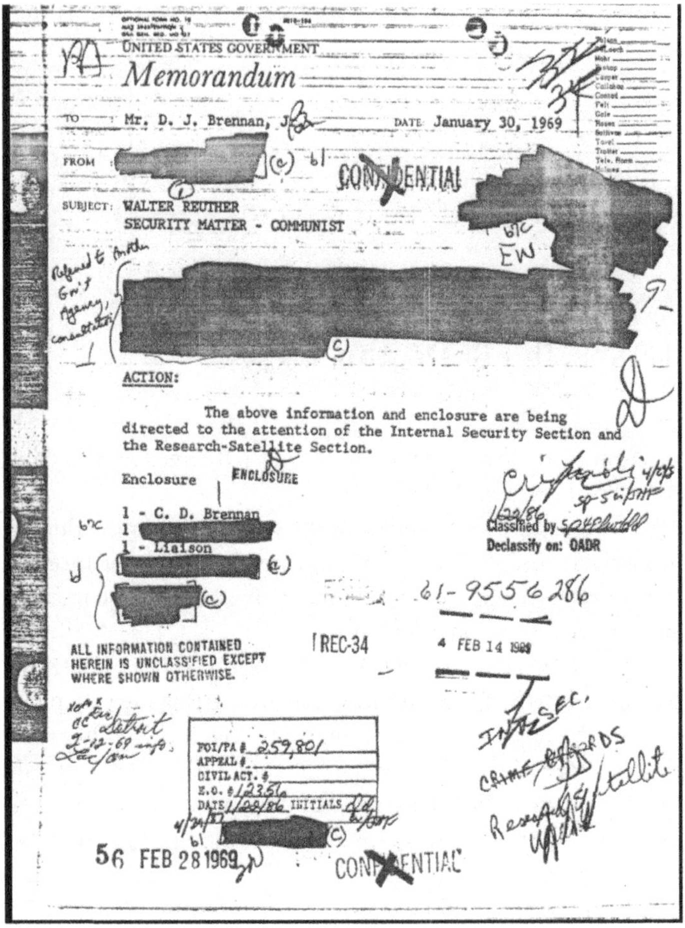

UNITED STATES GOVERNMENT

Memorandum

TO : Mr. D. J. Brennan, Jr. DATE: January 30, 1969

FROM : [redacted] (c) b1

CONFIDENTIAL

SUBJECT: WALTER REUTHER
SECURITY MATTER - COMMUNIST

[redacted] (c)

ACTION:

The above information and enclosure are being directed to the attention of the Internal Security Section and the Research-Satellite Section.

Enclosure ENCLOSURE

1 - C. D. Brennan
1 [redacted]
1 - Liaison
[redacted] (c)
[redacted] (c)

Classified by
Declassify on: OADR

61-9556286

REC-34 4 FEB 14 1969

ALL INFORMATION CONTAINED HEREIN IS UNCLASSIFIED EXCEPT WHERE SHOWN OTHERWISE.

FOI/PA # 259,801
APPEAL #
CIVIL ACT. #
E.O. # 12356
DATE 1/28/86 INITIALS

[redacted] (c)

56 FEB 28 1969

CONFIDENTIAL

New Left Movement. FBI memo between Brennan and Sullivan.

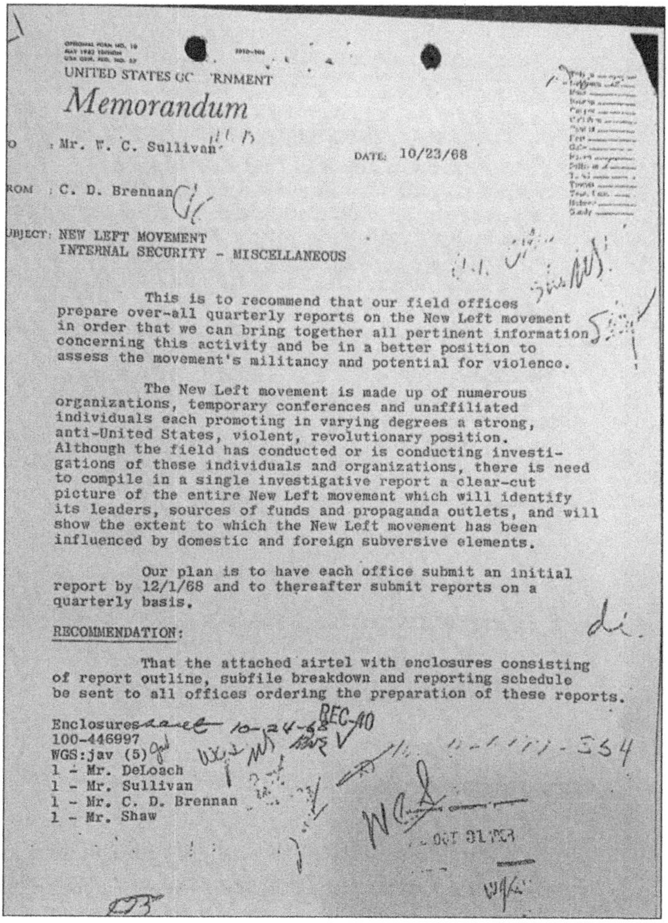

UNITED STATES GC 'RNMENT

Memorandum

TO : Mr. W. C. Sullivan

DATE: 10/23/68

FROM : C. D. Brennan

SUBJECT: NEW LEFT MOVEMENT
INTERNAL SECURITY - MISCELLANEOUS

This is to recommend that our field offices prepare over-all quarterly reports on the New Left movement in order that we can bring together all pertinent information concerning this activity and be in a better position to assess the movement's militancy and potential for violence.

The New Left movement is made up of numerous organizations, temporary conferences and unaffiliated individuals each promoting in varying degrees a strong, anti-United States, violent, revolutionary position. Although the field has conducted or is conducting investigations of these individuals and organizations, there is need to compile in a single investigative report a clear-cut picture of the entire New Left movement which will identify its leaders, sources of funds and propaganda outlets, and will show the extent to which the New Left movement has been influenced by domestic and foreign subversive elements.

Our plan is to have each office submit an initial report by 12/1/68 and to thereafter submit reports on a quarterly basis.

RECOMMENDATION:

That the attached airtel with enclosures consisting of report outline, subfile breakdown and reporting schedule be sent to all offices ordering the preparation of these reports.

Enclosures
100-446997
WGS:jav (5)
1 - Mr. DeLoach
1 - Mr. Sullivan
1 - Mr. C. D. Brennan
1 - Mr. Shaw

This memo was released due to the President John F. Kennedy Assassination Records Collection Act of 1992. It reveals that the FBI's Brennan and Sullivan collaborated on intelligence matters.

Anonymous Tip to the FBI Telephone about a "Contract" on Walter Reuther.

April 21, 1969

GENERAL INVESTIGATIVE DIVISION

Attached reports that anonymous telephone call was received by our Detroit Office from an unknown male. Caller stated a "contract" had been let on Walter Reuther to one [redacted] Appropriate local authorities and Reuther's security staff advised.

Bureau files contain no references identifiable with [redacted] Secret Service Headquarters advised. Detroit Office was instructed to advise Secret Service, Detroit. No FBI jurisdiction.

b7C
b7C

b7C [redacted]erg

ALL INFORMATION CONTAINED
HEREIN IS UNCLASSIFIED
DATE 1/22/86 BY SP4[illegible]

The Detroit FBI Field Office received this information on 4/21/1969 and shared it with the Secret Service. "67c" is a code granting exemption from disclosure through the Freedom of Information Act. The name of the person who allegedly received the contract is redacted.

Anonymous Threat LHM.

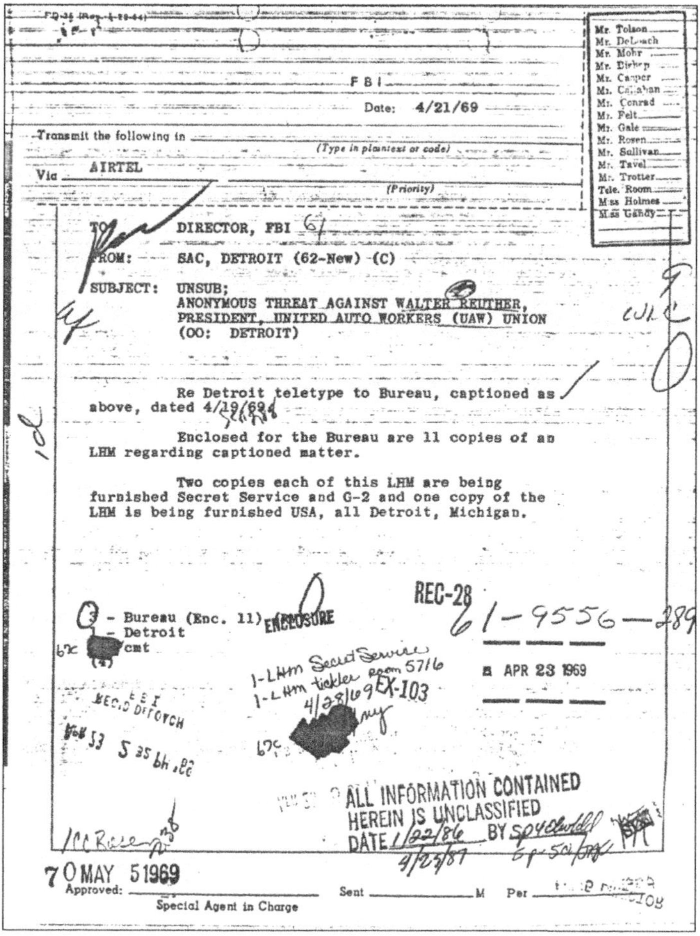

FD-36 (Rev. 5-22-64)

Mr. Tolson
Mr. DeLoach
Mr. Mohr
Mr. Bishop
Mr. Casper
Mr. Callahan
Mr. Conrad
Mr. Felt
Mr. Gale
Mr. Rosen
Mr. Sullivan
Mr. Tavel
Mr. Trotter
Tele. Room
Miss Holmes
Miss Gandy

FBI

Date: 4/21/69

Transmit the following in (Type in plaintext or code)

Via AIRTEL (Priority)

TO: DIRECTOR, FBI

FROM: SAC, DETROIT (62-New) (C)

SUBJECT: UNSUB; ANONYMOUS THREAT AGAINST WALTER REUTHER, PRESIDENT, UNITED AUTO WORKERS (UAW) UNION (OO: DETROIT)

Re Detroit teletype to Bureau, captioned as above, dated 4/19/69.

Enclosed for the Bureau are 11 copies of an LHM regarding captioned matter.

Two copies each of this LHM are being furnished Secret Service and G-2 and one copy of the LHM is being furnished USA, all Detroit, Michigan.

3 - Bureau (Enc. 11) ENCLOSURE
2 - Detroit
b7c [redacted] cmt
(4)

REC-28 61-9556-289

APR 23 1969

1-LHM Secret Service
1-LHM tickler room 5716
4/28/69 EX-103

b7c [redacted]

ALL INFORMATION CONTAINED HEREIN IS UNCLASSIFIED DATE 1/22/86 BY

70 MAY 5 1969

Approved: Special Agent in Charge

Sent M Per

The same day the FBI received the tip about a "contract" being let on Walter Reuther, they did an LHM, FBI code for a background check, on the person or persons named as having the contract. This was sent to the Secret Service and G-2 (Military Intelligence).

In the margin, a notation "ld" was written. 1(d) is a national security exemption to the Freedom of Information Act. A list of sixteen names and offices is in the upper corner of this document. One of those is Mr. Sullivan. Sullivan was Hoover's number-three man, assistant to him, and operationally in charge of all the Bureau's criminal, intelligence, and espionage investigations. Sullivan had overseen the FBI's in-house investigation of the JFK assassination. Sullivan was told to work closely with John Whitten, who was doing the CIA investigation. When Whitten learned the FBI had withheld documents from him, that CIA Director Richard Helms had not provided him with all the Agency's files, and that Oswald had been photographed at the Cuban consulate in Mexico City, he told Helms that this required more investigation. Helms removed him from the case and put James Angleton in charge of the investigation. The reports written by Sullivan and Angleton became the basis for some of the Warren Commission report.

In 1968, Sullivan was the lead FBI investigator in the assassination of Martin Luther King. Sullivan was also involved in the investigation of the assassination of Robert Kennedy. In August of 1971, he expressed major disagreements with Hoover over national security and suggested that Hoover should retire. Hoover refused and forced Sullivan out.

Sullivan had been scheduled to testify before the House Select Committee on Assassinations in December 1977. William Sullivan was shot dead near his home in Sugar Hill, New Hampshire, on 9th November 1977. Major Mason J. Butterfield, law enforcement director of the New Hampshire Fish and Game Department, said that Mr. Sullivan, who had been on the way to meet two hunting companions shortly near daybreak, had been shot and instantly killed by another hunter, Robert Daniels, Jr., 22, who had mistaken Mr. Sullivan for a deer. Mr. Daniels, son of a state policeman, pleaded no contest on Nov. 18 to a charge of shooting and killing a human being mistaken for game. Mr. Daniels was hunting with a rifle equipped with a telescopic sight when he shot Mr. Sullivan 20 minutes before sunrise. An inquest decided that he had been shot accidentally, and Daniels was fined $500 and lost his hunting license for 10 years. At the time of his death, Sullivan was working on a book with journalist Bill

Brown about his experiences. The Bureau: My Thirty Years in Hoover's FBI was published posthumously in 1979. In the book, Sullivan expresses skepticism that Lee Harvey Oswald, James Earl Ray, and Sirhan Sirhan acted alone. Mr. Sullivan was known both within the Bureau and by a wide and distinguished circle of acquaintances outside it as less a policeman than a scholar, one whose interests ranged from theoretical Marxism, on which he was an acknowledged expert, to modern English poetry. Sullivan held advanced degrees from American and George Washington Universities and an honorary doctorate from Boston College.[114]

Walter Reuther
Internal Security — Labor Matter December 10, 1969

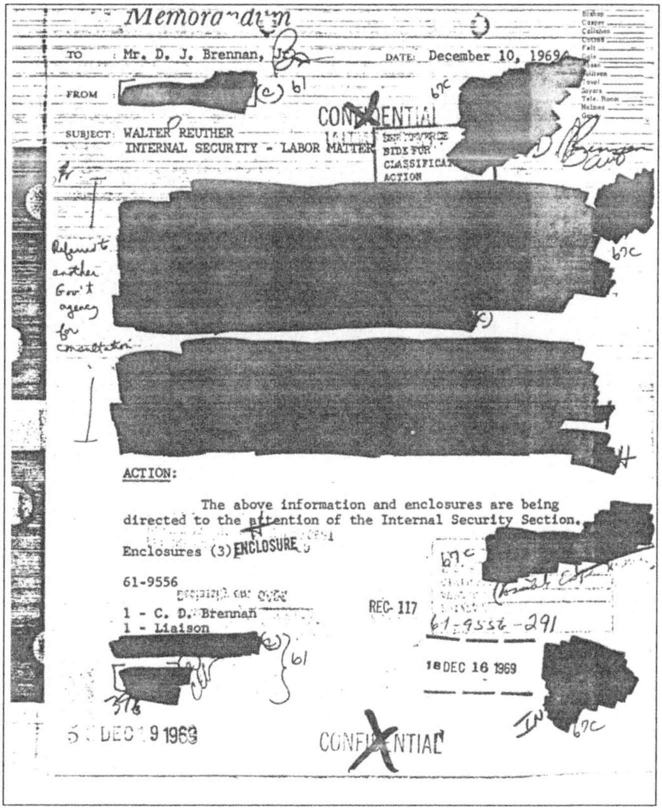
Memorandum

TO : Mr. D. J. Brennan, Jr. DATE: December 10, 1969

FROM : [redacted] (c) b1

CONFIDENTIAL

SUBJECT: WALTER REUTHER
INTERNAL SECURITY - LABOR MATTER

Referred to another Gov't agency for consultation

[redacted]

ACTION:

The above information and enclosures are being directed to the attention of the Internal Security Section.

Enclosures (3) ENCLOSURE

61-9556

1 - C. D. Brennan
1 - Liaison

[redacted]

REC-117

61-9556-291

18 DEC 16 1969

5 DEC 19 1969

CONFIDENTIAL

114 https://spartacus-educational.com/JFKsullivan.htm

The memo sent five months before Reuther's death is addressed to D. J. Brennan. The author's name is redacted for privacy and national security reasons. The entire body of the memo is redacted because it pertains to another government agency. A copy was sent to the same "Liaison" who received the Reuther—Communist memo from January 1969.[115]

The FBI's latest additions to the JFK Collection at the National Archives, resulting from a Trump Presidential Executive Order in 2025, include files that are well known to serious researchers of CIA-funded anti-Castro Cuban exile groups, such as the Directorio Revolucionario Estudiantil (DRE), usually known in English as the Cuban Student Directorate, and the Castro-friendly Fair Play for Cuba Committee (FPCC).

However, the latest versions of these records reveal the FBI's undue deference to the CIA in classifying its own records on surveillance inside the United States. More than 62 years ago, the FBI surrendered its domestic counterintelligence mandate to an agency supposedly responsible only for espionage outside U.S. borders, and it did so during the first official investigation into President John F. Kennedy's assassination and beyond. By examining both recently released FBI and CIA documents, JFK researchers have learned that the FBI acquiesced to the CIA's demands despite encroachment on the Bureau's domestic intelligence domain. JFK researchers have long become accustomed to the black redactions in FBI files, many of which appear to have deleted information permanently, with no unredacted version available. However, the handwritten notations "another United States Government agency" are found on fully declassified and newly located documents. That agency was the CIA.[116]

In the FBI's documents released to Bill Gallagher in the 1980s due to his FOIA request, 17 pages dated between 1967 and 1970 are listed as "Pages referred to other Government agencies for direct response or consultation." These are likely to have been classified by the CIA, and in 2025, the Bureau estimated it would take until 2028 for them to complete a FOIA request for four of them.

115 WJBK-TV Collection: Walter Reuther's FBI Files; FBI FOIA release No. 275,050; File No. 61-9556, Section 8, 1967-1970.Walter P. Reuther Library, Wayne State University, Detroit, MI

116 Chad Nagle, "From the JFK Files: FBI Ceded Domestic Intelligence Operations to CIA, "JFK Facts, April 21, 2025." https://jfkfacts.substack.com/p/from-the-jfk-files-fbi-ceded-domestic

Police notification to the FBI of a plane crash including Walter Reuther.

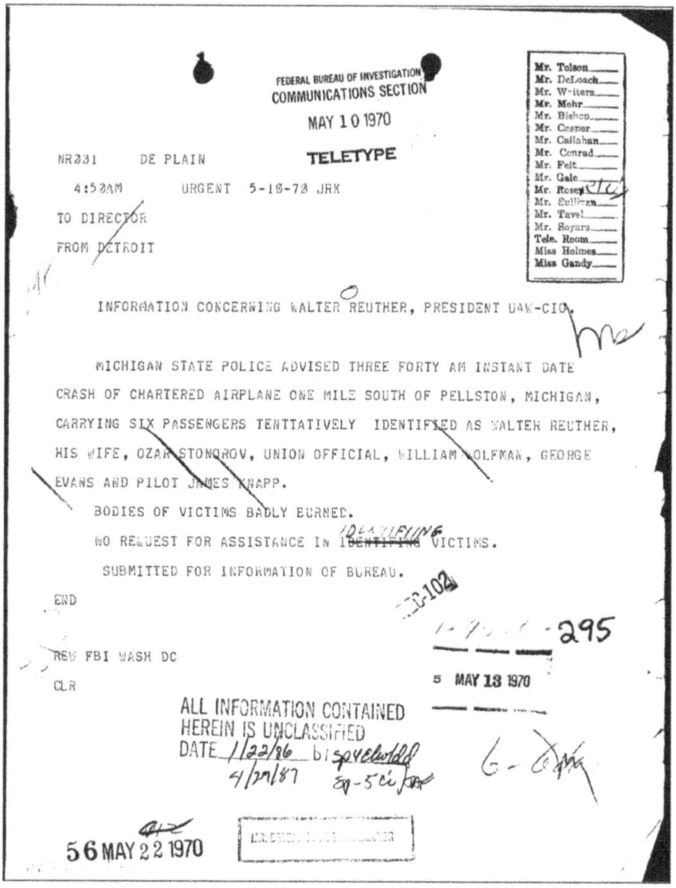
FEDERAL BUREAU OF INVESTIGATION
COMMUNICATIONS SECTION
MAY 10 1970
TELETYPE

Mr. Tolson
Mr. DeLoach
Mr. Walters
Mr. Mohr
Mr. Bishop
Mr. Casper
Mr. Callahan
Mr. Conrad
Mr. Felt
Mr. Gale
Mr. Rosen
Mr. Sullivan
Mr. Tavel
Mr. Soyars
Tele. Room
Miss Holmes
Miss Gandy

NR031 DE PLAIN

4:50AM URGENT 5-10-70 JRK

TO DIRECTOR

FROM DETROIT

INFORMATION CONCERNING WALTER REUTHER, PRESIDENT UAW-CIO.

MICHIGAN STATE POLICE ADVISED THREE FORTY AM INSTANT DATE CRASH OF CHARTERED AIRPLANE ONE MILE SOUTH OF PELLSTON, MICHIGAN, CARRYING SIX PASSENGERS TENTTATIVELY IDENTIFIED AS WALTER REUTHER, HIS WIFE, OZAR STONOROV, UNION OFFICIAL, WILLIAM WOLFMAN, GEORGE EVANS AND PILOT JAMES KNAPP.

BODIES OF VICTIMS BADLY BURNED.

NO REQUEST FOR ASSISTANCE IN ~~IDENTIFING~~ IDENTIFYING VICTIMS.

SUBMITTED FOR INFORMATION OF BUREAU.

END

REW FBI WASH DC

CLR

-295

5 MAY 13 1970

ALL INFORMATION CONTAINED
HEREIN IS UNCLASSIFIED
DATE 1/22/86 BY

56 MAY 22 1970

The Michigan State Police sent a notification to the FBI at 3:40 am on May 10, advising them of a plane crash that included, among the deceased, Walter Reuther. At 4:50 am, the Detroit FBI office sent an urgent teletype to FBI Director J. Edgar Hoover, informing him. Copies were sent to seventeen others, including Sullivan. This was the same group that was notified of the "contract" let on Reuther the previous year. In the next few hours, three other communications followed this memo.

Appendix III. The Barfield Instrument Corporation and Kollsman Instrument Reports

After retrieving the captain's altimeter from the wreckage of the Reuther crash, William Weston, a NTSB field investigator, first took the altimeter to Barfield Instrument Corporation on May 19, 1970.

One of Barfield's findings was that: "One of the set screws was out of the rocking shaft, allowing the calibration arm assembly to be loose in the shaft. There was an indentation adjacent to the missing set screw hole. The set screw, which was missing from the rocking shaft, was recovered from within the case. Inspection revealed charred aluminum in the brass screw threads. The rocking shaft screw hole was inspected and found to have the threads torn out." Barfield summarized the inspection writing:

In conclusion our opinions are:

A. The lack of any broken pivots or jewels and the generally good condition of all gear and pinion teeth tend to indicate that initial impact was not severe.

B. The bent rocking shafts were apparently the result of crushing the case from the side.

C. Most damage to the instrument was the result of intense heat.

D. The condition of 'the front gear mechanism would indicate that the observed barometric setting of 29.75 was not altered as a result of the crash.

E. The gear and pinion mesh starting with the long pointer back through the intermediate wheel and pinion assembly was intact and. operative. Beyond that point, the gearing was all disengaged.

Photo 19 [in the Kollsman Report] shows the altimeter mechanism with the case placed over it.

Weston then took the altimeter to Kollsman Instruments in Elmhurst, New York (the instrument manufacturer) for further examination and testing on May 26 and 27, 1970. Attending the investigation were Mr. William Weston (NTSB), Mr. Ted Cymmer (FAA — May 27 only), Mr. Jolm Stanislaw (Executive Jet Aviation), Mr. James Angus (Kollsman), and Mr. Peter Redmond (Kollsman). After May 27, the unit was left at Kollsman for further investigation by Kollsman personnel. It was later returned to the NTSB along with the report. They took photos throughout the disassembly and examination of the altimeter.

Weston testified at the 1973 civil action by the Reuther Estate against the Emmett County Airport, saying that Kollsman found:

> "Concerning the condition of the set screw, it appeared that the threads in the hole were torn, and I think that's pretty visible on [photos] 24, 25...there's deformation of the threads. It would put an unnatural torque on the thing..."

The screw did not fall out due to worn or damaged threads. Photographs of the set screw showed normal threading. However, the screw hole shaft had its threads "torn" or drilled out, which caused the screw to slowly pull out as the flight progressed. This was consistent with the indentation mark near the screw hole, resembling a mark left by a high-speed drill bit that had drilled in the wrong area and then quickly retracted. The proper hole was located, and the threads were drilled out. The set screw was reinstalled. The altimeter seemed intact, despite being tampered with. As the rocking arm rotated, incorrect information would be sent to the altimeter's pressure capsule dials.

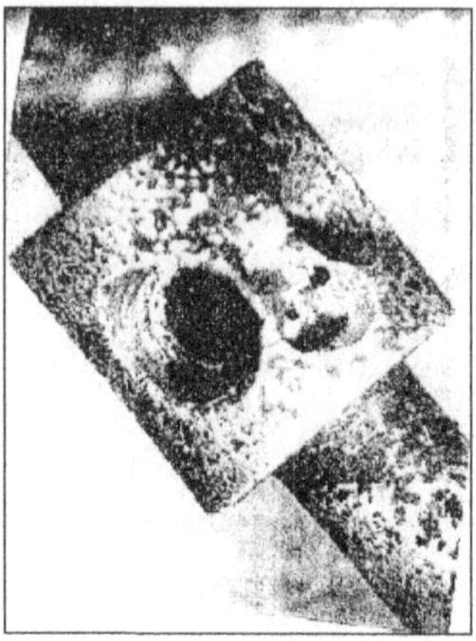

Physical damage adjacent to
the screw hole. [Kollsman Report]

Thread comparison with similar rocking shaft.
[Kollsman Report]

"Examination of a similar rocking shaft exposed to 1100°F, believed to be higher than that which the subject instrument was exposed to, showed that with a thread which is unabused and with a properly tightened screw,

a) the screw did not come out, due to the high temperature exposure,

b) there is an aluminum deposit on the brass screw threads under load,

c) the thread in the shaft tapped hole, Photo 39, is not damaged to the extent shown on Photos 24, 25, 26 and 27..."

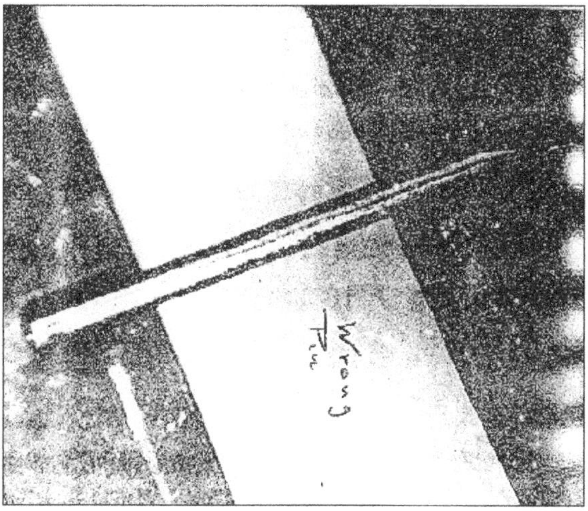

"Wrong pin..." [Kollsman Report]

"...it was a pin, but it was out of another altimeter."

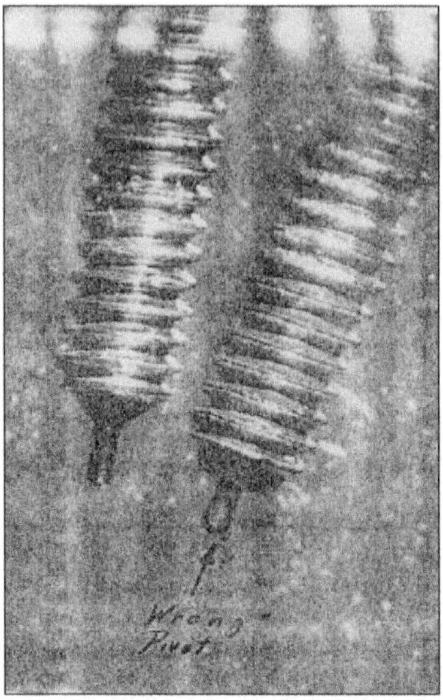

"Wrong pivot." [Kollsman Report]

"One of the pivots supporting the rocking shaft's rear was incorrect in that it is intended for a ring stone application only."

"Photo 37 shows the opposite end of the shaft showing the unit missing the end stone and also the ring jewel pushed off center." [Kollsman Report]

The end stone is missing, the ring jewel is pushed off center.

Discussion Transcribed from the Kollsman Instrument Report

No identification was present to trace the specific instrument type and date of manufacture.

The mechanism construction isolated the unit to one of three major types, each of which had numerous variations, none of which were TSO certified. All of these types were essentially military.

Careful study of the display elements and mechanism elements using a 30X microscope did not reveal any markings which would lead to a probable instrument reading at breakup.

The questionable calibration arm set screw is reasoned to have been in position at the time the X-ray pictures were taken and the stains on the calibration arm indicate that the arm position was reasonably correct.

If the questionable calibration arm set screws were loose at the time of the approach under concern, the instrument would probably indicated high by roughly 225 to 250 feet.

Considerable reinspection of altimeters of the same repair history is recommended to ensure that the altimeters in service are in accordance with the manufacturer's recommended standards regarding parts used, assembly techniques and calibration/compensation.

Author's Information Requests to NTSB

In 2024, I sent emails to National Transportation Safety Board Media Relations and, after getting no response, to the NTSB Office of the Inspector General, noting this:

Greetings,

Between 2018 and 2021, I filed three FOIA requests with the NTSB concerning a plane crash on May 9, 1970, near Pellston, MI.

FOIA-2018-00306
FOIA-2021-00253
FOIA-2021-00254

— I received a written response dated August 9, 2021. To summarize:

...Therefore, other than the brief accident report, available at this link: DCA70AZ008 (ntsb.gov), and the published aircraft accident report, AAR-71-03.pdf (ntsb.gov), shows no other records responsive to your request.

I now know this is an untrue statement. I have the Kollsman Instrument report on the altimeter in the plane during the crash. A researcher found it in the NTSB archives in 1992. I also have a 350-page deposition from William B. Weston in a civil suit filed by the Reuther Estate v the County of Emmett, MI (and others in civil actions in the Eastern District of Pennsylvania) on July 24, 1973.

Weston was the lead NTSB investigator for the instruments group. The NTSB's final report omitted the information that the altimeter had been made for the military, had no identifying marks, and had not been approved for use in civilian aviation. The accident report said the altimeter was reading 225 feet too high during the crash due to multiple defects.

I plan on publishing this in the near future. Do you have any comments or explanations?

Best,
Rob McKenzie

I received no response from the NTSB.

Image Credits

pp. 1-101. All photos courtesy of the Walter P. Reuther Library, Archives of Labor and Urban Affairs, Wayne State University, unless otherwise specified.

p. 56. Map of the Pellston, MI airport. NTSB accident report. National Transportation Safety Board Aircraft Accident Report, "Executive Jet Aviation Inc. Lear Jet L23A N434EJ Near Emmet County Airport Pellston, MI." May 9, 1970. Attachment No. 1, p. 1.

pp. 125-134. FBI documents. WJBK-TV Collection. Walter Reuther's FBI Files, FBI FOIA release No. 275,050, File No. 61-9556, Secion 8, 1967-1970. Walter P. Reuther Library, Wayne State Univerity, Detroit, MI.

pp. 135-141. Barsdale and Kollsman Reports. These photos were unearthed by AJ Weberman, who found them in an NTSB archive in Washington, D.C., in 1992. The NTSB currently denies having such photos.

Acknowledgments

After my first book, *El Golpe: U.S. Labor, the CIA, and the Coup at Ford in Mexico*, was published, I began researching the Walter Reuther plane crash and his death in 1970. I started by submitting a Freedom of Information Act request to the FBI for the classified documents they had on the crash. I also contacted Bill Gallagher, a reporter from Detroit Public Television, regarding his successful efforts in the 1980s to obtain FBI documents related to Reuther. Gallagher provided valuable insights into these records.

Podcaster and radio show host Ed Opperman connected me with A.J. Weberman, who researched the Reuther plane crash in the 1990s. After a lengthy phone call, Weberman shared all his files with me. These files included the elusive Kollsman Instrument report on the altimeter, which I had been unable to find. Weberman's documents also led me to David Norris, a private investigator hired by Walter's daughter, Elisabeth Reuther Dickmeyer, in the 1990s to look into the crash. Norris informed me about the court documents he couldn't obtain and provided contact information for Bruce Dickmeyer, Walter's son-in-law. Bruce and Elisabeth have kept a constant vigil regarding Walter's life over many decades. The Dickmeyers, Scott Houldieson, and Jeff Schuhrke helped obtain the Reuther Estate civil suit documents. Angie Stonorov Foster shared her thoughts on the Reuthers and their relationship with the Stonorov family. Additionally, Immanuel Ness offered valuable feedback on my initial attempt to write about Reuther's death and encouraged me to expand my article into a book-length work.

These people's generosity, insights, and support made writing this book possible. I am deeply grateful for their sharing of firsthand accounts and personal stories, which added a human dimension to the historical events covered in these pages. Their trust and openness gave me a perspective that no document alone could offer.

Rob McKenzie

Bibliography

Agee, Phillip. *Inside the Company: CIA Diary.* Bantam Books edition February 1976.

Barnard, John, *American Vanguard: The United Auto Workers during the Reuther Years, 1935-1970,* Wayne State University Press, 2004

Barnard, John, *American Vanguard: The United Auto workers during the Reuther Years, 1935-1970,* Wayne State University Press 2004

Bernstein. Harry, "V. Reuther Links CIA, AFL-CIO," *Washington Post*, May 23, 1966.

Braden, Thomas W. "Why I'm Glad the CIA is 'Immoral.'" *The Saturday Evening Post*, 20 May 1967

Carew Anthony. *American Labour's Cold War Abroad From Deep Freeze to Détente, 1945-1970.* AU Press, Athabasca University 2018.

Central Intelligence Agency, "1973-03-07. Air America, Inc. Vientiane, Laos Facilities and Operations," 197307 pdf. General CIA Records. Freedom of Information Act. Electronic Reading Room

Dickmeyer, Elisabeth Reuther, *Putting the World Together: My Father Walter Reuther: The Liberal Warrior*, LivingForce Publishing, 2004.

FBI Freedom of Information Privacy Act Request No.: 1543705-000

Fontes, Paulo and Larrissa R. Corrêa. *Labor and Dictatorship in Brazil: A Historiographical Review CPDOC*/FGV, Rio de Janeiro and Pontifícia Universidade Católica, Rio de Janeiro

Foy, David A. *Loyalty First: The Life and Times of Charles A. Willoughby, MacArthur's Chief Intelligence Officer.* Havertown, Pennsylvania: Casemate Publishers 2023

Griffin, Tom, *State–Private Networks and Intelligence Theory From Cold War Liberalism to Neoconservatism.* Routledge, 2022

Halberstam, David. *The Reckoning.* A Thomas Congdon Book, 1986.

Holusha, John, "Union Rebel. Jerry Tucker—The Man Who Is Fighting the U.A.W. from Inside," *New York Times*, October 23, 1988.

Interview with Stephen I. Schlossberg. The Association for Diplomatic Studies and Training, Foreign Affairs, *Oral History Project*, Labor Series, Interviewed by Morris Weisz. Initial interview date: June 25, 1993

Jacobsen, Annie. *AREA 51: An Uncensored History of America's Top Secret Military Base.* Little, Brown and Company, 2012

Klaber, William and Philip Melanson, *SHADOW PLAY: The Unsolved Murder of Robert F. Kennedy*. St. Martin's Press, 2018

Knapp, George, "Famed aviator John Lear, 79, departs on 'his next adventure'." April 1, 2022

Kollsman Instrument Corporation report on the altimeter conducted on May 26 and 27, 1970. Those in attendance: Mr. William Weston (NTSB), Ted Cymmer (FAA May 27 only), Mr. John Stanislaw (Executive Jet Inc), Mr. James Angus (Kollsman), Mr. Peter Redmond (Kollsman). Unpublished

Kuzmarov, Jeremy. "Did J. Edgar Hoover Order the Assassination of Martin Luther King Jr?". *Covert Action Magazine*, April 4, 2004

LA Times–Washington Post News Service, "CIA Linked to AFL-CIO Foreign Unit," May 23, 1966.

Lichtenstein, Nelson and Harold Meyers, "The Autoworker Who Transformed California," *The American Prospect.* November 25, 2022

Lichtenstein, Nelson. *The Most Dangerous Man in Detroit.* BasicBooks, a division of HarperCollins. 1995

Morgan, Ted. *A Covert Life: Jay Lovestone Communist, Anti-Communist, and Spymaster.* Random House, 1999

Morley, Jefferson. *The Ghost: The Secret Life of CIA Spymaster James Jesus Angleton.* St. Martin's Press, 2017

Nagle, Chad. "From the JFK Files: FBI Ceded Domestic Intelligence Operations to CIA," JFK Facts, April 21, 2025. https://jfkfacts.substack.com/p/from-the-jfk-files-fbi-ceded-domestic

National Transportation Safety Board Aircraft Accident Report. Executive Jet Aviation Inc. "Lear Jet L23A N434EJ Near Emmet County Airport Pellston, MI, May 9, 1970."

O'Sullivan, Shane, *Who Killed Bobby: The Unsolved Murder of Bobby Kennedy*, SkyHorse Publishing 2008

Parenti, Michael and Peggy Norton, "The Wonderful Life and Strange Death of Walter Reuther," *Covert Action Quarterly*, 1995 No. 54 p. 43.

Reuther, Victor G., *The Brothers Reuther and the Story of the UAW/A Memoir.* Houghton Mifflin, 1979

Romualdi, Serafino. *Presidents And Peons: Recollections of a Labor Ambassador in Latin America.* Funk & Wagnalls. 1967

Russell, Dick, *The Man Who Knew Too Much.* Carroll & Graf Publishers, 1992

Schuhrke, Jeff "'Comradely Brainwashing': International Development, Labor Education, and Industrial Relations in the Cold War," *Labor. Studies in Working-Class History*, Volume 16, Issue 3 (September 2019), pp. 39–43, 49, DOI 10.1215/15476715-7569788.

Schuhrke, Jeff, *Blue Collar Empire: The Untold Story of US Labor's Global Anti Communist Crusade.* Verso, 2024

Smyth, Donald, *The Road Less Traveled; A Biographical Sketch of Stephen I. Schlossberg — A Trade Union Life.*Peppertree Press, 2009

State of Michigan for the Circuit Court of the County of Emmet, Irving J. Bluestone, Administrator with the Will Annexed of Walter P. Reuther and Irving J. Bluestone, Administrator with the Will Annexed of the Estate of May W. Reuther. Civil Action No. 173-3, Deposition of Clarence Tatro

UCLA Library Center for Oral History Research. Interview with Paul Schrade. Tape X, Side One. June 5, 1990

UCLA Library Center for Oral History Research. Interview with Paul Schrade. Tape X, Side Two

UCLA Library Center for Oral History Research. Interview with Paul Schrade. Tape XI, Side One July 24, 1990

United States District Court Southern District of New York. Dr. Morgan N. Reynolds, on behalf of The United States of America Plaintiff, vs. Science Applications International Corp. et al., Defendants. State of Nevada: County of Clark Affidavit ECF Case 07 CIV 4612 (GBD) January 28, 2008

Weberman, A.J. "Did Nixon Run a Domestic Operation Phoenix? Fatal 'Accidents' During the Nixon Administration." https://educationforum.ipbhost.com/topic/15078-was-joe-biden-the-target-of-a-botched-assassination-attempt-by-cia%E2%80%99s-domestic-operation-phoenix-component/?tab=comments#comment-175317

Welch, Cliff. "Labor Internationalism: U.S. Involvement in Brazilian Unions *1945–1965.*" *Latin American Research Review* Vol. 30 No.2.

Wikipedia. John Lear. https://en.wikipedia.org/wiki/John Lear, and https:/en.wikipedia.org/wiki/John_Lear; https://www.8newsnow.com/

investigators/famed-aviator-john-lear-79-departs-on-his-next-adventure/

Wiles, Richard, "Union man killed in Pellston plane crash: Accident or Conspiracy?" May 2015, *Mackinac Journal*

Wilford, Hugh. *The Mighty Wurlitzer. How The CIA Played America.* Harvard University Press. 2008.

Wilford, Hugh. *The CIA: An Imperial History*. Basic Books, 2024

WJBK-TV Collection. Walter Reuther's FBI Files, FBI FOIA release No. 275,050; File No. 61-9556, Section 8, 1967–1970. Walter P. Reuther Library, Wayne State University, Detroit, MI

Index

Made in the USA
Monee, IL
08 November 2026

67384908R00100